THE MURDER OF THE CHURCH SECRETARY

By

D.J. Parsons

THIS STORY IS DEDICATED

TO

SECRETARIES

The Letter **where the story begins...**

TO WHOM IT MAY CONCERN:

For the Reason That:
A two-thirds vote of the U.S. Senate is required before an impeached person can be forcibly removed from office. This is not possible in our current state of the Union; and

For the Reason That:
Most incumbents seek re-election, and their historical likelihood of winning subsequent elections exceeds 90%; and

For the Reason That:
All 100 U.S. State Senators to the United States of America and all 435 House of Representative Congressmen/Congresswomen, including the President of the Senate and the Speaker of the House, have not been able to find a way to harmonize our various racial, religious and cultural diversity, our many walks of life and professions, our mannerisms and expressions, and our multitude of opinions where compromise is required; and

For the Reason That;
  Unaccountability to the People of the United States of America for crimes of Congress;

We the People of the United States of America find the 112th United States Congress GUILTY OF TREASON.

The 112th United States Congress (Defendant) is Sentenced as follows:
  To be left to the Conscience and Ability of each of the 15,000 persons randomly commissioned *and* selected by computer lottery, *and* by receiving *this Letter* to:

Select a Person belonging to one of the following Institutions who have committed crimes against the United States:

  a. U.S. Senate
  b. U.S. House of Representative
  c. U.S. Judicial
    i. Judges
    ii. Lawyers
  d. Political Financiers including Corrupt Lobbyist
    i. Corporate and Private Monies

NOT TO INCLUDE:
  The President of the United States of America.

It is entirely up to you, THE COMMISSIONED DELEGATE, to eliminate in any way you see fit any person or atrocity committed by one the above.

MAY THE HOUSE CLEANING BEGIN.

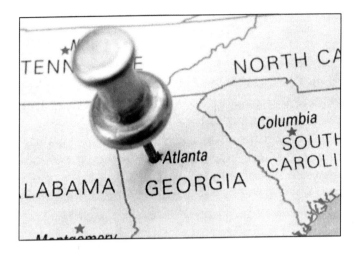

THE ASSASSINS MAP

(Found in Dr. Stan Anders apartment in Atlanta)

THE DISABLED ASSASSIN
SANTA MARIA, CA

Glenn E. Colton resided fifteen minutes from his workplace in an expensive subdivision in Santa Maria, California. Santa Maria stretched from the coast inland to valleys growing corn, celery, lettuce, and broccoli, to the tune of five million packages of produce a year.

Promotions didn't always land in a handicapped man's lap, but Colton's warm personality, coupled with his quick wit and excellent foresight, had been rewarded. As Vice President at International Food Products, a 70,000 sq. ft. state-of-the-art cooling center, his job was to interface between the docks at the Port of Long Beach, and the incoming product from Nogales.

Framed pictures of his grandchildren stood where his wife placed them over ten years ago, before the horrid hospital stays and her passing. Although his social life was adequate, the smell of lilacs and the sound of his wife's laughter were never far. Old army missions were never far from his mind, either. Almost every day, Glenn E. Colton would say to himself, and to others, "Annie and America – my two loves."

The Letter

Was it a hoax?

The Letter came on white bond paper with no return address or identifiable markings. He tossed it aside with the rest of the junk mail. Nevertheless, Colton couldn't get rid of *the letter's* nagging questions. *Is the United States over? Have we destroyed ourselves, with no hope of turning us around?* Someone had gone to a great deal of trouble, someone clever and driven. He chewed on *the letter's* proposition all night.

Should he do it? Would he do it? Could he do it, at **his** age, a man with a handicap sign hanging from his rearview mirror? After strapping on his legs the two braces that had allowed him to walk for the past 30 years, he rummaged for keys to a locked gun case, and began to gather his resolve.

THE SENATOR
STATE CAPITOL PARKING
SACRAMENTO, CA

The dangerous thing about wrong thinking was that after a while, it became the only way you knew how to think. Like many other politicians, California Senator Robert McDaniel had mastered the art of giving only the appearance of getting something done, and would do so at any cost. When the Senator entered into an alliance with a corrupt transportation deputy at the border, he began to accumulate great amounts of untaxed money in offshore accounts.

No one cared enough about Senator McDaniel to warn him of the precipice on which his soul teetered. His "better than thou gloat" over a piggish face was detestable to all, even his constituents. It was not surprising that the black Mercedes went unnoticed until the lot emptied. A Capitol Security Guard recoiled after leaning into the blown-out driver's side window, frantically wiping blood off of his hands.

On an adjacent rooftop, a man in a dark suit pulled back. Was it the chill of the wind, or the reality of what he had just done? Summoning his legs, he stumbled toward the rental with the handicapped plates.

THE GUNRUNNER
NOGALES, AZ

The arrangement with the Senator had been straightforward. The transportation deputy turned gunrunner, and his underlings, would unload the produce from Mexico; then, reload the empty containers returning to Mexico with grenade launchers, portable anti-aircraft missile systems, recoilless rifles, and sometimes explosives. As a member of the Violent Crime Impact Committee, the Senator's part of the bargain would be to watch for surprise tip-off check points. Aware of the gunrunning out of Nogales, the ATF had been unable to pinpoint the leak.

****

The older man with the braces checked out of the motel on the outskirts of Tucson and drove south. If all went well, he'd be back in Santa Maria by nightfall. The first mission went well if you did not consider the Senator's blood all over the wheel, and the car window. Colton burned his clothes, ditched the rental, and threw his disguise into the ocean.

The transportation deputy did think it was odd a V.P. from International Foods wanted to meet with him, but had no idea Colton was on to them. The news of the Senator's car shooting had not been released to the media. If International Foods had any idea of the missing shipping manifests, they would not have sent that crippled old man. He underestimated the Vietnam Vet who did not use a gun this time, but a wire.

****

He felt little guilt. Was it his fault *the letter* came the same day he discovered a United States Senator was using HIS company to sell illegal firearms to Mexico? His source at the docks had been able to trace the fraudulent manifests to the gunrunner back to the Senator. The corrupt Senator's railings about other people's immorality was all it took to convince Glenn E. Colton *the letter* was not a coincidence, but maybe even God-ordained.

As it was, it was easy enough to push the Senator's partner at the border out of the car on the way north through Yuma.

THE SLEUTH
LAKE OZARK, MO

A new marriage and move to the country meant changes in Mae Lancaster's employment, and months of job hunting resulted in nothing. Eventually, a church in a nearby city advertised for a secretary at the same time of renewed rumors of *"the end of the age is approaching."* That was how business woman Mae Millan-Lancaster found herself on the front lines of organized religion.

Although Mae's past entrepreneurial endeavors gave her only enough money to scratch by on, she had saved enough to set up a nice office a few miles from their lake home, a place for her to get away to. Her husband built the small studio-office-cabin with a deck overlooking the lake. A new sound system and old record albums sat sandwiched between her computer and treadmill, with a kitchenette and half bath at the back.

Bible commentaries, maps, Hebraic prophesy, copies of codices and papyrus, and pictures of archeological artifacts filled her bookcases to replace *How to Make a Million Dollars With Your Ideas* and *Women and the Business Game* on her shelves.

Mae paused to admire an ancient map. *You can spend your entire life studying, and only scratch the surface,* she mused.

What did the past five years of research reveal? The Dead Sea Scrolls had been found including all the Old Testament books except Esther; Sodom had been excavated and evidence showed it had been destroyed by a high degree of temperature; and scientists claim discovery of King Herod's tomb.

She returned to the present. *The trick to pull off my meeting in Lynchburg will be to have the song director cover for me at the church, and make sure John has a full refrigerator.* Mae e-mailed her best friend Dominique Findley of her upcoming interview with the head of the largest Christian publisher in the nation.

THE PET-LOVING PONIES MAN
LEXINGTON, KY

The Kentucky Horse Racing Commission, the KHRC, an independent state agency with the responsibility to keep the sport honest and safe, regulated steroids, crop rules, licenses, and standards for animal welfare.

People with power and money hated regulations, and Ray Bucks Derrick, KHRC Record Custodian, was under investigation.

The press release dangled from Record Custodian Derrick's fingertips, indicating the imminent joint meeting between the Rules and Drug committees. The agenda had been set for a vote to be taken regarding the disclosures needed for additional regulatory violations. The inside information he had been leaking to the Supreme Court Chief Justice would be uncovered and the judge knew it.

Backed into a corner, Derrick was nervous. *That old fart on the Supreme Court had the absolute nerve to call down here and threaten me? Blackmail ME?? After I have lined his pockets for years? Cold day in hell! Where IS that letter? Where is that letter!*

The Letter

Untouched, *the letter* sat on his side table all evening. *It couldn't be real...stupid pranksters,* he concluded, and then pitched it.

That night he couldn't sleep. Two o'clock in the morning, three o'clock in the morning, four o'clock; tightening his robe, he slipped downstairs. He peeked through the empty cat food cans and coffee grounds. What he needed was a drink.

With a lit cigarette and the bottle of vodka, Derrick turned on his copier and straightened the crumpled wad. As he settled into his executive chair, at his executive desk, with its exquisite executive desk ornaments, a cat appeared in the doorway of his study.

****

Arson! Oh, he wasn't going to do the deed himself; he had been given a name. At the right time, he would leave the racetrack, and drive northeast to Bethesda.

Ray Bucks Derrick pulled the road atlas from his desk and said to the Siamese studying him from the top of a bookcase, "Let's see, Erasmus. What's the best route to Washington, D.C.? This *house cleaning* is going to happen with or without us; why not make it our way out, too?"

Erasmus stretched, and meowed in agreement.

THE GAMBLING CHIEF JUSTICE
BETHESDA, MD

It cost a lot of money to keep up appearances, live in expensive homes, attend galas, send children to private schools, and belong to pricy country clubs. A Chief Justice's annual salary was currently set at $223,500, and the eight Associate Justices annual salary was $213,900. Not quite enough for some.

The Supreme Court of the United States was the highest judicial body in the United States. They were nominated by the President and appointed after confirmation by the Senate. Justices of the Supreme Court had life tenure. Since 1970, the average length of service had increased to about twenty-six years. There was not much that could be done to rid the country of a Supreme Court Judge, if he or she had been corrupted.

I have to stop gambling! I hate to gamble, however Olivia's addicted and I'm addicted to Olivia. I do it for her. I wish she was dead. Hmmm…She could be. The way out of this mess is to pay the money. The way I can pay the money is if I call the Kentucky Racing Committee and threaten that Record Custodian. No one will know. Then I'm out. O-U-T Out!

As it turned out, Conservative Supreme Court Chief Justice Thom Hopkins was O-U-T. His house burnt down, with him in it, that very night. Not much to identify.

THE ARSONIST
BETHESDA, MD

Joel L. Moore was indicted of twenty-eight counts of first-degree murder after being accused of setting fire to a downtown Hilton in Lubbock County, Texas in the early 1980s. He was not seen setting the fire; however, a hotel employee saw him in a stairwell and identified him carrying what she described as "a can of lighter fluid." By the time of his trial, the witness was nowhere to be found, with the trial ending in a hung jury.

In 1995, Moore was arrested in Atlanta for the arson-murder of his wife, Tammy. Prosecutors stated he knocked her out before setting the fire. This time, the prosecution was unable to find an expert to support their theory of the crime. In 2008, he was once again in front of a jury in an obvious insurance fraud, but the crime lab in Houston found no evidence of gasoline. Pyromania wasn't the only compulsion of Moore, he also played the ponies.

Ray Bucks Derrick and Joel L. Moore met once when the victim's name and instructions were given. "It must look like an accident. No one except the judge can be in the house, especially not the pets," Derrick directed.

****

Moore entered Chief Justice Thom Hopkins' house through the wine cellar, disabling an alarm system a second-year television technician could have managed. The Arson Investigator ruled the fire accidental, finding a cigarette had been lit beside an electric stove burner, alongside of a spilled bottle of rum. The kitchen fire spread through the house uninterrupted, and sedatives were found in the judge's autopsy.

Other notable clues were that the judge's wife had been called away to their children's home on a false alarm, and their Persian pedigree cat and Standard Poodle were missing.

THE HUSBAND
THE COUNTRY CLUB PLAZA
KANSAS CITY, MO

The construction crew watched the twenty ton crane hoist the 10,000-pound compressor up and over and through electrical lines, in through a small ninth story window. On the ground, a dozen men in hard hats clapped and whistled. The crane operator, John Lancaster, stepped down from the cab and modestly said, "Hey, guys, anyone can do it."

Brawny and handsome John swung the rigger pads up onto the crane, hooked the wrecking ball to the front end of the chassis and removed the crane's counterweights. With a few inches to spare between buildings, using his rearview mirrors, he backed out of the alley, and headed back to the yard.

"I hope that's the last job ticket," he muttered. His boss had a way of cramming in as many jobs as possible on Fridays, knowing he was trying to get out of Kansas City, and on the road south to the lake, and to Mae.

After three failed marriages, all he could do was shake his head and wonder how he ever married again. Mae Millan's A-frame sat nestled in the woods secluded on five acres. After a year of driving back and forth from the marina, on a double-dare by his friends, curiosity about the woman he had been hearing so much about got the best of him. A cruise down her half-hidden driveway, on a Saturday five years ago, revealed an attractive woman on a John Deere, mowing in her bathing suit. There would be no second date with this woman unless he was prepared to take her on full-time with five dogs, four cats, and a bird. By the end of the summer, he began fixing up her A-frame to sell.

He knew his wife had done all she could to blend into her husband's life. She was now a thirty-eight-year-old church secretary and never been married. He didn't know a lot about her past; however, he was able to piece together a time in New York as a fashion designer. She once confided she walked away from thousands of dollars of sewing equipment, lots of dreams, and lots of disappointments, a long time ago.

But what concerned John most was his wife's recent obsession with world events. With TERROR STRIKES HOME headlines taped to her office walls, and stacks of articles about strange weather patterns, plagues and famines, baffled John's attitude was, *I'm just an ordinary guy. I still believe the United States is the most wonderful, powerful country in the world. What is she worried about?*

As his red F250 pulled onto I-70 heading south toward the Ozarks, usually level-headed John Lancaster, was irritable, apprehensive and hungry, a bad combination to have if you were John Lancaster.

THE GOVERNOR'S MANSION
TALLAHASSEE, FL

Scott Randall was a third-rate, third-generation southern politician. His father was serving in the House of Representatives and his grandfather was involved in local politics in Jacksonville, where the Randall name was more feared than admired. The seat of politics had been handed to Scott Randall as it had been handed to his father before him; and, he hated his family for it.

This predestination made it mandatory for Randall to not only give up talent as an artist, but also trade the girl he loved for a woman with more appropriate breeding. The future Governor of Florida was left with a conscience riddled with guilt.

On this particular morning, the Governor made plans to take the Porsche down to Apalachicola into the National Forest to paint. He made all the arrangements to clear his calendar, pay off his bodyguard to lay low, and was not expected back for at least two days.

Two days, a week, two weeks, and still no governor.

THE WALL STREET ASSASSIN
NEW YORK, NY

After years of Wall Street luring top commodity traders with outrageous bonuses, the recent financial regulations had been forcing the most talented brokers to flee for bigger money. Last year, a Switzerland-based commodities giant made overnight billionaires of a handful of senior traders.

Harry Walden was the Chief Financial Officer of BOND-ON TRADING and had always considered himself an honest man, as well as a successful trader. (He would not have been involved with an ex-junk-bond magnate who blurred the lines in their high-risk, high-reward speculative dealings, if his wife had not been hit by a taxi in a freak accident.) His wife's dying breath had been to beg her husband to forgive the man. *It was an accident,* she had said.

The Letter

After the junk bond fiasco, with the consequences of $10 million in fines and another $35 million in lawsuits, Walden took the fall for his company and spent the last few years in federal prison. With an empty house to come home to, as well as barred from anything to do with banking, he had two goals his first day out: make an appointment with his barber, and take a second look at *the letter* he found delivered to his post office box.

As chance had it, Harry Walden DID know of a corrupt governor; and, there was that business about Barbara.

****

His sister, Barbara Walden-Jones, had confided in him. Her fiancé, now thirteen years later the Governor of Florida, was canceling their engagement, and marrying someone in his own social circle. She was three months pregnant. Walden wanted to do what all older brothers want to do: kill the man. "You just can't go out and kill a man, can you?" he asked that day. He was, however, able to help his sister by financing a boutique in Boca Raton, a fancy women's store that catered to shoppers hopping back and forth to the Bahamas.

How old is Barbara's Randie now? He reminisced. *It's been so long since Randall dumped her. What's the saying? You Reap What you Sow?* After dwelling on the mysterious *letter*, Walden made a few calls. *If I had to pay for MY sins, shouldn't everybody?*

DISCARDED
BOCA RATON, FL

Barbara opened the *Pompano Beach Gazette* and strained her eyes at the headlines. *MISSING – FLORIDA GOVERNOR SCOTT RANDALL!* The Governor, the story continued, disappeared during a two-day hiatus, and the FBI had been called in to aid state investigators. Police were swarming all over the state.

Not consciously knowing why, she bolted to check on her teenage daughter. "Ouch!" A fingernail broke down to the quick as she opened the sliding glass door that led to their pool. The painful index finger throbbed as she watched her daughter, Randie, swim laps. Lingering just long enough to survey the shrubs and fence line for anything out of the ordinary, she went back into the house.

****

There had not been a day that went by that she had not thought about Scott Randall. After all, her daughter looked like him. Instead of her mother's big blue eyes and platinum blond hair, her daughter sported her father's penetrating deep brown eyes, dark curly hair, and unfortunately that nose. Luckily, her daughter inherited her mother's tiny frame, and the nose was cute; the boys were swarming.

Barbara returned to her sun room, and poured herself a glass of Chardonnay. As she gazed out onto the ocean, she recalled that horrible day of long ago; the place they would meet in the National Forest at Apalachee Bay to watch him paint. She never could reach down deep enough to hate, but felt only disappointment in Governor Scott Randall. *What a shame. What a waste. A weak man,* she thought, rehashing the days and nights of anguish after his betrayal. He was a man without the fortitude to stand up to the Randall Clan, the powerful southern plantation family who reached back two centuries.

He offered money, as general cads always do, but she had refused, sticking to an excellence of character instead. *"Don't worry,"* she had said. *"There won't be any trouble."*

And with that said, Barbara Walden changed her name to Barbara Jones, relocated to the other side of Florida, and gave birth to a six pound baby girl she named, "Randie."

A DROWNING SORROW

The Governor loved his small cabin on the outskirts of the Apalachicola River where he came to unwind, the one source of joy in the man's life. An unfamiliar feeling came over him as he climbed to the loft to unpack. *Has someone been in here?* After a quick look around, his eyes settled on the dresser. *Are the drawers ajar?* He descended on the stairs uneasy. *Has a chair been moved? Hadn't there been a full bottle of Gin?*

It wasn't until that evening that he found the photograph of a young, dark-haired girl posing in a beach cover-up, tucked under a candy dish. "THAT doesn't belong here," the Governor shouted. *Who is she? There's something about her. Do I know her?* "Curious," he said, replacing the girl's picture on the table.

****

The river had been Scott Randall's place to go to paint for years. In the evenings, he would load his portable easel onto the houseboat, motor out a fair distance, and using water colors paint sunsets from the boat. This night the waves were unusually rough.

There was no way of knowing how much time passed in concentrating and sketching, sketching and concentrating, perturbed about the mysterious photograph, until he felt the squish in his tennis shoes. *"Damn! My feet are cold. NO! WET!! What the hell?"* He splashed over to the dashboard, and turned the key. The ignition started. "Thank you, Lord," spilled off of the Governor's tongue, only as a saying, not really meaning it.

His confidence was short lived, however. The engine abruptly stopped, and the boat went quiet. *Won't start! Won't start! Water deeper. Water deeper.* "The damn thing is going to sink," he screamed with no one to hear. Terrified he reached for the radio only to stare in disbelief at its dangling wires. A mad dash to the boat's storage bin revealed the inflatable raft was missing.

There were three notions on Governor Scott Randall's mind as the houseboat disappeared into the Apalachicola River that flowed into the Apalachee Bay. One—the girl in the picture had his nose, the Randall nose. Two—he never learned to swim. And three— he could pray for help, but he had never believed it was important to establish a relationship with God, *why would God hear him now?*

THE PUBLISHER
ETERNAL HOUSE OF PUBLISHING
LYNCHBURG, VA

Dr. Warren Peterson had been a lucky guy. He married his high school sweetheart, and they had four boys. To be a minister sometimes meant being broke your whole life; as the saying went...*you keep him humble Lord...and we'll keep him poor.*

When the opportunity to head up the largest Christian publishing company in the U.S. came his way, with a six-figure salary, Warren jumped at the chance to remove himself from what had become a monotonous and oftentimes hypocritical routine. His wife, Julie, always followed Warren's lead, the kids were grown, and the golf course was calling. He had done his share of weddings and funerals. Only the Lord knew what was happening in the world, so what could HE possibly do more than he had done already? This new job was a desk job: a business as any other. BIG business! Thirty-five million in annual sales, and a complex covering a city block, not to mention his face on the cover of an occasional magazine. This was it. This was the life. He couldn't knock the smile off.

A DIVIDED ALLEGIANCE
ETERNAL HOUSE OF PUBLISHING
LYNCHBURG, VA

Connie Bryan had been a secretary twenty years; it was a thankless job. Oh, you were thanked all right; however, vases of flowers and well wishes were gestures you couldn't take to the bank. As it turned out, Connie was luckier than the average secretary because she and Warren Peterson went way back. As Warren was promoted up the ministerial ladder, he brought Connie with him. Once they were locked together in a retreat cabin, and after all the years of working together, and telling each other their secrets, the escapade culminated in love-making neither of them could forget. The campus maintenance man was able to jimmy the lock, and in due time, they were rescued. It never happened again, and except for a special glance once or twice a year, Dr. Warren Peterson maintained his boss, husband and father role, and Connie remained his right-hand friend and confidant.

The evening Connie caught Warren going through Dr. Stan Anders' desk, and watched him scurry back to his own office carrying a few files, she didn't think much about it, except that it was unusual. Not until Warren disappeared did Connie think about it again.

TRADING IN INFLUENCE
STATE CAPITOL
MONTGOMERY, AL

The ethics and morality of lobbying was a dual-edged sword. Lobbying was often spoken of as corrupting the law in order to serve a particular interest. Another side of lobbying was making sure others' interests were defended against others' corruption. The question was — who were the good lobbyists and who were bad ones?

Lobbyist Danielle Ashton had her hooks into a congressman well known to sell his vote. Somewhere along the way, lines were crossed from attempting to influence his decision, to downright bribery. Not any small deal. Worldwide, bribery alone was estimated to involve over one trillion U.S. dollars annually. Both Danielle Ashton and Alabama Congressman Frank Shaw got rich pressuring the EPA for stricter emissions limits on industrial equipment in Alabama.

There was one problem — the good 'ol boys network had been leaning on Congressman Shaw to flip his vote in favor of the Industrial Equipment lobby, and the midnight trysts with sexy and alluring Ms. Ashton had grown stale.

THE DOUBLECROSS
BIRMINGHAM, AL

Danielle looked stunning in her black crepe jumpsuit and white satin jacket. She looked at her diamond Rolex.

"Another martini, Ms. Ashton?" asked her favorite waitress in the lounge area of the Airport Top of the Crown Hotel.

"Yes, I'll wait a little longer, thank you, Jill," Danielle replied.

The daughter of a single-parent African-American librarian, Danielle Ashton had a Caucasian father who left when she was two years old. Her mother was frugal and smart, however, and the two of them had all they needed. Danielle grew into a beautiful woman, and her mother's good job enabled her daughter to attend the best schools and rise to the top.

However, getting involved with misappropriated funds, and corrupt bidding landed her in the middle of the unholy alliance between corrupt business and corrupt politics; and like quicksand, she couldn't get out. One thing led to another, and falling in love with a married congressman from Mobile was the final mistake that took her all the way under.

Hours later and still alone, nursing her third martini, Danielle looked out, down and over the twenty stories to the blinking city night lights of Birmingham below. *He has made me his fool.*

The Letter

Back at her penthouse apartment, she kicked off her heels and ran a hot bath. The predicament she found herself in was beginning to dawn on her. Not just awkward, but dangerous. Her hands were cold and trembled as she sorted through her mail. *What's this? This letter is strange.*

The tub warmed her and the blue pill calmed her. She chose the flannel pajamas she always wore when frightened, and turned on headline news. Wrapped in her grandmother's afghan, Danielle burrowed into the overstuffed couch and reached for *the letter. Is it a sign? How could I do it? If I don't do it, Frank could blackmail me, forever. Would he? Of course he would.*

She would be ruined, and the congressman was too powerful to accuse him of anything. Too many knew they had been lovers, and the old double standard was alive and well— indiscretions acceptable for him, but not for her.

Through tearful eyes, she could hear her mother's warnings of the corruption of money. *Oh, Mother, I need you tonight...to talk as we used to do.* When it had been just the two of them, their favorite saying was, *It's only you and me, babe.*

Except it was only her now; at least her mother wasn't around to be ashamed of her. Danielle thumped the letter with her manicured nails, and said to the anchor on the television news, "If it is him or me—it's not going to be ME!"

A FUNERAL
MARS HILL CEMETERY
WASHINGTON, DC

"Mars Hill is my favorite historical Washington cemetery," said President Saundra Adams to FBI Agent Glenda Wiley, as their caravan entered the thirty-five acres of historic burial ground founded in 1807. She didn't liked funerals, except as an avid history buff. *You can't get any more historical than dead members of Congress, military, and beloved heroes of our country,* she mused as she swung her long legs out of the presidential Lincoln Town Car.

The first female President made it a point to attend the Mars Hill Chapel at Christmas when stories were read of Christmases past, caroling, and the best hot chocolate in the nation was served. The President had also recently visited Mars Hill to make an appearance at the dedication ceremony of two park benches honoring the names of several of the signers of the Declaration of Independence.

Agent Wiley nudged the President through the crowd toward the covered area reserved for family and high government officials. Bringing the President's mind back to the task at hand, the Agent said, "It's not every day a Supreme Court Chief Justice dies in a terrible fire."

STAN ANDERS, DOCTOR OF MINISTRY
RELIGIOUS COLLEGE
ATLANTA, GA

His responsibilities at the publishing company in Lynchburg became unimportant after Anders' wife finally left him, and he took the post in Atlanta. "My buddy, Warren, thinks he's always right," accused Dr. Stan Anders, Doctor of Ministry. "Warren doesn't appear to care about what is going on in America."

A religious scholar with several books to his credit, the Doctor's mind snapped some time a few years back. "We are in the midst of evil," he declared in front of his class.

Sometimes religious people could no longer hold up under their own inner spiritual battles. The more one demanded holiness, the greater the hypocrisy, and hypocrisy was motivated by egotism. The more Dr. Stan Anders pointed out the sins of others, the more he slipped away from Jesus Christ's teachings. The hollow blackness in his eyes revealed emptiness, and worse yet, one eye drifted. A demon had made his home there, with hatred consuming any light he may once have had.

"We have caught almost all our government leaders in a lie. We are letting undocumented workers steal from us. Women are sluts and homosexuals are deviants. Human nature does not change, my friends. The Bible tells us in Ecclesiastes there is nothing new under the sun.

We cannot reform ourselves. Every now and then, God starts over." Anders' damaged ego soared out of control; his mouth had become cruel, as he spoke.

Several weeks prior, at a makeshift table in a small apartment on the outskirts of Atlanta, the Doctor had sat down to compose *the letter* that began a revolution. He had selected at random, by computer lottery, fifteen thousand names to invite into his crusade.

Dr. Stan Anders was going to help God out a little.

A MYSTERY TO SOLVE
ETERNAL HOUSE OF PUBLISHING
LYNCHBURG, VA

Stan Anders was Warren Peterson's best friend; had been his best man at Warren's wedding, and substitute preached for him on many occasions. There were no questions asked when Warren selected Stan to head the marketing division of the publishing company.

No one saw the nightmare coming. Life was going so well. It was sheer coincidence, or divine appointment, as they said, when Warren caught a glimpse of Stan walking out of an Atlanta hotel restaurant, and climb into a black SUV with an obvious foreign man, maybe Indian? Iranian?

****

Warren's schedule was full and he wasn't supposed to be in Atlanta that day. Connie had put through the call. One of his friends from old seminary days died, and the funeral was the following day.

The funeral was filled with people from both the religious and political arenas. Warren never cared for the rumors that circulated for years around his old classmate. When he knew the man, his classmate was a simple pastor in rural Mississippi, but blessings began to dry up for this minister-turned-politician. "I HAVE to go," Warren explained to his wife while packing an overnight bag. "He was my roommate. And good heavens, honey, the man was electrocuted!"

****

"Hey, Stan, who was that guy you were with at the Atlanta Hilton?" questioned Warren a few days later back in Lynchburg.

Stan denied the meeting.

****

Warren would have never checked up on his friend, and colleague, Dr. Stan Anders. However, Accounting reported a great deal of unexplained travel; California, Arizona, Washington, Kentucky, and now Florida.

Since Stan had been working out of his Atlanta office more often than not, on gut instinct, Warren made the decision to glance around Stan's office at the publishing company the first chance he could get, after everyone was out of the building.

The occasion presented itself right away.

THE HUNT

A brief look at the office did not reveal anything out of the ordinary, except there was a laptop was on the desk. *Stan never goes anywhere without his laptop.* Warren deliberated.

Stan had inadvertently shared his computer password with Warren at a meeting regarding new security issues a few months prior. Warren concentrated to recall the conversation. As chance had it, a stack of blank disks were nearby.

As he scanned through Stan's documents he began to perspire. "I really must be nervous about finding something I shouldn't," he whispered to himself, wiping his brow with a monogrammed handkerchief his wife had given him for his birthday.

One file did stand out among others as unusual. Words, names, and locations began to flash and scamper across the screen. As far as he could see, nothing was recognizable or related to his publishing company. He was looking at a list of some kind, but a list of *what? Hmmm...a list of cities and states?* Warren copied the file onto a disk he had already placed into the drive, and had become relaxed enough to think he was getting away with the unnerving spying on his friend, when...*what was that? Someone was coming!*

He closed the laptop. *Connie. What is she doing here this late?* He grabbed a few files to divert any attention to the disk he held in his hand, and made a quick exit through the back corridor, through the conference room. *Slow down. Look calm. Breathe normal.*

Back in his own office, *I have the right to be in Stan's office, don't I? After all, I am the president of the company, aren't I?* Dr. Warren Peterson continued to justify himself.

And now he had a disk.

A LOVING CONFRONTATION
ETERNAL HOUSE OF PUBLISHING OFFICES

"I need to see you after you are caught up in there," Connie called out to Warren, as he hurried by her desk on the way to his own.

"Why, what's up?" inquired Warren, not meeting his secretary's eyes.

"Well, okay, iiiifffff this is a good time...I'll come in right nowwww," Connie said with sarcasm. She stood up, entered Warren Peterson's executive office, and closed the door.

Alarmed, Warren's eyes grew wide, "Is there anything wrong, Connie?"

"Oh, come off it, Warren, No... not with ME, but I've had a bad feeling about YOU for several days," Connie said. With a sharper tone, she continued, "What's wrong with you?"

Warren loosened his tie. "Oh Connie, Connie, calm down and sit down. Want a Coke?"

"No, I don't want a Coke, but if you have anything stronger in that locked credenza of yours, I'll have one of those," she said.

Caught as usual, Warren put on his "I'm the Boss" face. "Connie, I can't tell you anything. Yes, there may be something, I don't know enough myself. It may not concern you...or me. Thank you for your concern. I'll holler if there is something you can do." Warren looked guilty, and pretended to stack papers.

Connie knew a dismissal when she heard one. This was not the time to press. "Okay, sure," said Connie with one eyebrow up.

After his secretary was back at her desk, Warren sauntered over to their connecting glass window. Separating the mini-blinds, he whispered, "Connie, my love, whatever you do, let this one go."

But Warren Peterson knew better. He was well acquainted with that eyebrow, and when the brow went up, Connie Bryan had no intentions of backing off.

A WEST COAST BURIAL
THE SECRET SERVICE AGENT

President Saundra Adams was careful not to make friends with the Secret Service; however, Agent Glenda Wiley had earned a special place. The Secret Service investigated thousands of threats to the President each year. Because of a thorough investigation by Agent Wiley, a valuable piece of information had been revealed, aiding the Secret Service in averting what could have been an incident.

Glenda's smart, eleven-year-old daughter, Kassi, sat watching her mother pack for yet another out-of-town funeral. "Mom, what's going on in the government? This is your fourth funeral. Is someone picking you off one by one?" Kassi snickered. "That's goofy, Mom."

With the dog barking and her daughter at the front door waving and throwing kisses, Agent Wiley was whisked away by a two-star Deputy Chief in a uniformed division cruiser. In the back seat, all the way to the White House, she fidgeted. *What in the hell is the matter with me?* The morning traffic was jammed. Her "something's wrong" inner bells were ringing. Air Force One would land in San Francisco for Senator Robert McDaniel's memorial service, three weeks after his death. The family had decided against a traditional funeral, it would have needed to be closed-casket. Washington

FBI and San Francisco FBI were rendezvousing. After all, it had been a homicide.

Her daughter's innocent comment stuck in her brain. *No, it couldn't be. Could it?* Secret Service Agent Glenda Wiley felt her SIG Sauer P229 pistol chambered and ready in her loose-fitting jacket.

LANCASTER HOME
LAKESIDE HEIGHTS
LAKE OZARK, MO

"Look, I can make decisions around here, too, ya know!" Mae said with annoyance. "Everyone should have enough provisions to survive several months, maybe YEARS! I see it will be up to ME to prepare us for what's coming, and there was a sale on those canned goods," she added in defiance.

John and Mae Lancaster argued often. Few people thought alike, but the couple had been considering that maybe they weren't so happy after all. Harsh words started over something unimportant, the dogs, cats, his mother, or Mae's growing obsession with world events, then ended with a knock-down drag-out.

John felt he was doing HIS share. He worked hard building fences, and a huge, insulated, heated and air-conditioned metal building for the dogs. He did not complain about the kitty litter on the bottom of his feet in the downstairs bathroom. He did have to admit his mother was difficult, however, John's real concern was his wife's paranoia, and her constant nagging, *The sky is falling…the sky is falling.*

****

This particular day, he and the boys were sitting around belting back a beer at the marina before heading home. Much to his dismay, he had begun to admit his wife's predictions had been coming to pass. America's jobs HAD disappeared, the weather patterns WERE unusual, and differences in political views were causing good friends to begin to avoid each other.

"Oh, come on John, calm down. Don't take life so serious. The economy will bounce back. It always does," his friends advised.

"I'm out of here," John called back over his shoulder. "I'll be over to help pour concrete tomorrow."

John Lancaster came home complaining about the barking dogs, and sulked over the $500 in canned goods he tripped over, stacked inside the front door.

A FRIENDSHIP
DOMINIQUE FINDLEY

Dominique Findley and Mae Lancaster had been friends since Girl Scouts. They had seen each other through Dominique's numerous love affairs, and Mae's many business failures. (Dominique Findley recently moved back from Colorado, the best and longest of friends.)

"Do you have the cigs?" asked Mae.

"Sure do! Do you have the sandwiches and dark beer?" asked Dominique.

"Yes, but I'm not sure about this horse trip thing," complained Mae for the third time.

Dominique spoke with a pronounced calmness. "Relax. We're ready. They are saddling the horses, and the wrangler will be here. Quit worrying and have a good time."

With Dominique, Mae could always come up with a game plan, and she was indeed in need of encouragement before the trip next week to the publisher in Virginia, the trip someone was covering for her at the church so she could go; the trip her husband didn't know about yet.

The Ozark hills were not the mountains Dominique Findley were used to in her beloved Colorado, nevertheless the trail ride she chose for the outing was going to be fun, anyway. Or so she thought. The ride up into the hills went smoothly until they reached the top.

"Off the horses!" the wrangler instructed.

"What?" questioned Mae.

"OFF the horses!" the wrangler shouted, this time with more authority. Dark clouds began to gather.

An angry thunderstorm blew through, but their gear kept them dry, the sun soon peeked out, and they were able to enjoy their picnic. Mae marveled, *the view is beautiful; God's beautiful world. Could it be so fragile as to hinge on just one domino; one dirty bomb, one earthquake or volcano, one nutcase?*

The trio returned to the stables. Mae said, "Thanks, Domi. You always come through."

"No problemo," Dominique replied. "And don't worry; go do your thing out there at that publishing company. Be yourself, you know what you're doing."

"Get me off this horse," shouted Mae. The horse picked up into a gallop and horse and rider flew down the trail, with Mae dodging tree branches.

If Mae Lancaster had known what events were soon to follow, she would have stayed on the hillside, even on that horse.

J. EDGAR HOOVER BUILDING
WASHINGTON, DC

"A senator assassinated in California with no leads in the investigation, and a Supreme Court judge dies in a suspicious fire, a few days apart? AND NOW A MISSING GOVERNOR?" shouted FBI Director Matthew Conway.

"Might not have anything to do with the President," commented the Chief of Staff. "We have all three locations under surveillance; nothing yet."

FBI Operations Agent Kamber Jeanes always cleared her throat as she was about to add something overlooked by her superiors. "I believe we do have some leads," she began. "The ATF has been working a gun trafficking case in Nogales. U.S. Customs and Border Protection reported one of theirs found at the bottom of a cliff; the man's neck had been cut with a wire of some kind." The Agent continued, not taking a breath, "…and late last night I received a report from our field office in Atlanta. That minister who ran for the Senate several years ago had a run-in with some power lines, fried to a crisp."

"Get the Director of National Intelligence, pronto," FBI Director Matthew Conway ordered. "We need to brief the President."

THE CONFESSION
ETERNAL HOUSE OF PUBLISHING

"What in the world are you up to, Stan?" yelled Warren. "Why are you going on those trips? Why the secrecy? I don't know who you are anymore!"

Stan responded, "Keep out of it, Warren. I'm sorry you had to stick your nose in. I won't be able to warn you again. Don't get mixed up in this. Once this thing started, I had to go along."

"Go along. Go along with WHAT?" Warren shrugged his shoulders and waved his hands.

"Warren, the Church Age is over. We have become country clubs concerned only with who has the best music or better facilities. I had always felt I was doing God's work, you know, blessed are they that mourn over the grief of sin? Everything that is ugly and black in contrast to God's goodness? Yet I've screwed up; bad, unforgivable." Anders wanted to go on with a well-rehearsed speech, but Warren interrupted.

"Stan. Sit down. Put those boxes down. Where are you going? What have you done?" Exhausted, Warren collapsed onto the couch.

"Forget it, Warren. There is too much to tell, and I don't have the time. Know this. Stay away from me. I thought I knew what I was doing, but it's too late to undo what I'm responsible for. STAY OUT OF IT!"

Dr. Stan Anders picked up his personal desk items, including the picture of his wife, and walked out of his office.

GRAND NATIONAL ASSEMBLY BUILDING
ANKARA, REPUBLIC OF TURKEY

Turkey was a democratic, secular, constitutional republic with an ancient cultural heritage. Since there had been a threat shared by all countries by the Soviet Union in our not so long ago history, there had been close relations with Washington, and Turkey had benefited from U.S. support.

Early in her Presidency, Saundra Adams received disturbing complaints about Turkey regarding Human Rights violations; torture, women's rights issues, and press freedom. After the President called the Turkish Prime Minister to ask about these subjects, both came away with a mutual understanding. President Adams had been made to feel she could call the Turkish Prime Minister, and vice versa, without either having to flex their power, to get something accomplished.

President Saundra Adams answered the direct line from the President of the Republic, the Head of State himself, and readied herself for nothing less than a catastrophe. After all, Turkey had close political, cultural, and economic relations with the Middle East, and bordered Iran, Iraq, and Syria.

"Yes, Mr. President, thank you, I am well, and you?" President Saundra Adams maneuvered through the appropriate protocol. "How can the United States aid you today?" she continued, knowing all the National Security Agency recording equipment was crackling and popping.

"It's not what you can do for us, Madam President; it is what has come to our attention in Istanbul YOU need to be aware of, Madam President. The Prime Minister will brief you at this time. Good day, Madam President." The President of Turkey was gone and her friend, the Prime Minister connected.

"Khaleel, what's happened?" she questioned her ally.

The Prime Minister began—

"Our Ministry of Internal Surveillance has picked up chatter. One of our most wanted criminals has been seen with an American on Turkish soil. Your American is now missing, however, the criminal has been arrested carrying what appears to be a very dangerous document. We are transmitting the document direct to Langley, now."

"Khaleel, give the short version," the President instructed.

"It's *a letter* of some kind."

CIA – FOR YOUR EYES ONLY
LETTER – confiscated from Turkish Terrorist

TO WHOM IT MAY CONCERN:

For the Reason That:
A two-thirds vote of the U.S. Senate is required before an impeached person can be forcibly removed from office. This is not possible in our current state of the Union; and

For the Reason That:
Most incumbents seek re-election, and their historical likelihood of winning subsequent elections exceeds 90%; and

For the Reason That:
All 100 U.S. State Senators to the United States of America and all 435 House of Representative Congressmen/ Congresswomen, including the President of the Senate and the Speaker of the House, have not been able to find a way to harmonize our various racial, religious and cultural diversity, our many walks of life and professions, our mannerisms and expressions, and our multitude of opinions where compromise is required; and

For the Reason That;
Unaccountability to the People of the United States of America for crimes of Congress;

We the People of the United States of America find the 112th United States Congress GUILTY OF TREASON.

The 112th United States Congress (Defendant) is Sentenced as follows:
To be left to the Conscience and Ability of each of the 15,000 persons randomly commissioned ***and*** selected by computer lottery, ***and*** by receiving *this Letter* to:

Select a Person belonging to one of the following Institutions who have committed crimes against the United States:

> a. U.S. Senate
> b. U.S. House of Representative
> c. U.S. Judicial
>> ii. Judges
>> iii. Lawyers
> d. Political Financiers including Corrupt Lobbyist
>> iv. Corporate and Private Monies

NOT TO INCLUDE:
The President of the United States of America.

It is entirely up to you, THE COMMISSIONED DELEGATE, to eliminate in any way you see fit any person or atrocity committed by one the above.

MAY THE HOUSE CLEANING BEGIN.

CIA HEADQUARTERS
MCLEAN, VA

President Adams cleared her morning to accompany FBI Director Conway over to the George Bush Center for Intelligence, to join CIA Director Carter Elliott in viewing the suspicious document the Prime Minister of Turkey described as *a letter*. With Agent Wiley at her side, it had been agreed the less commotion at the White House the better, until they knew what they were dealing with.

The primary function of the CIA was to collect information about foreign governments, corporations, and individuals, and advise. Sometimes they engaged in covert affairs at the request of the President when an emergency field operation might be required, for the immediate suppression of a threat. Also, they were sometimes used instead of military, to avoid a declaration of war.

CIA Director Elliott handed each in the room a copy of *the letter*, and took his place at the podium. "The original document from Turkey is on its way via private jet, direct to the FBI Lab for DNA analysis, latent prints, and any other trace evidence. We know it is a nut-case zealot; however, we don't know the why."

The FBI Director stood. "Well, that's not quite true, Carter. *The letter* explicitly states government corruption is the *Why*."

"As to the *where,* we know multiple locations are being used for the murders," contributed Counterterrorism Specialist Lon Munson.

"The *How* seems to be random, nothing to link the murders," added the CIA Director.

"*Who* could be random, too," said President Adams.

The conference lasted less than an hour. "We have 20,000 employees in the FBI costing the taxpayers $8 billion a year; and, we have 33,000 employees at the CIA with only God knows how much we're spending, because that amount is classified," recited President Saundra Adams, standing to indicate the meeting was over. "Here's the deal. Someone out there is going to be murdered, as we speak. I have the utmost faith in our national security. Go to work. Agent Wiley will see me back to the White House."

As the dark sedan with tinted windows pulled out of the CIA parking lot, Agent Wiley said to the President, "You're going to have to stop jetting around without the full Secret Service Detail; the two of us are taking a great risk driving alone like this, Madam President."

President Adams' arms were crossed, and her frown lines were showing.

CROSS TIMBERS CHURCH
LAKE OZARK, MO
SUNDAY

When they said, "You can turn back the page to your life's last chapter, and not remember it," they were right. Mae looked in the mirror to see a pretty woman, but not the glamorous woman she used to be. She was glad to not run in the fast lane anymore, although she did miss its clarity—at least in business she knew who the sharks were. Not so in her new job as a church secretary. Nevertheless, she did love it. As it turned out, it was the secretary who kept the office running in harmony, put out fires, encouraged the low, sympathized with the sad, and prayed with the ones who needed the One.

The church switchboard brought Mae back to the present. "Yes, I'll be here a few more minutes. You can stop by and give me the music to copy. Yes, I have the copies of the Homebound Ministry Schedule. Oh, by the way, how is your grandson? Has he recuperated from his broken arm?"

At three o'clock in the afternoon, Mae Lancaster went on her rounds. Bibles and hymnals back to the pews, check the Fellowship Hall, empty trash, and lock the pastor's office, leaving messages taped to his chair. She stopped on her way through the sanctuary to gaze on her favorite mural. As the story went, when the shepherd had a lamb always getting lost, the shepherd broke its leg in order to teach it. But then CARRIED THE LAMB.

"He Ain't Heavy, He's My Brother ," Mae hummed as she closed up the church, and turned the key in the lock.

GOING FISHIN'
SUNDAY AFTERNOON

The wild scenic part of the Rogue River, known for its steelhead fly fishing, brought Bud Kennedy to Grants Pass every year and John Lancaster had been meaning to go. The usual routine was Phil Hanson, a pilot from Arkansas, flew up in his four-seater Cessna 182, and landed in Lincoln, Missouri to pick them up. The rules were one piece of luggage, no toiletries or women.

"The Rogue River on the Oregon Coast is the place for spring salmon," boasted John's friend, Bud.

"You're gonna talk for days about the feeling from the first strike of the morning to the last rise on a run, we do it the old school way passed down from generations of Oregon steelhead fisherman," Phil, the pilot added.

"Count me in! I've been making my own dinners, anyway," said John.

MAE'S DESTINATION, OR, DESTINY
MONDAY

Mae spoke with Dr. Peterson's secretary twice.

"Yes, Mrs. Lancaster, Dr. Peterson is looking forward to talking with you regarding the women's survey you have taken," confirmed Connie Bryan. "He has received your reference letters and transcript, and knows you come recommended."

Kindred spirits, Mae Lancaster and Connie Bryan hit it off. Their phone conversation lasted over an hour as they exchanged opinions on everything from global warming, to Israel, to earthquakes, or, if Nostradamus was really trying to tell the world something. Connie Bryan put Mae at ease regarding the upcoming interview with the publisher. "Yes, I'll make sure you make your flight home, Mrs. Lancaster," she promised.

The groundwork was set. Mae had all her facts; her back-up unarguable; and the good news kept coming.

John agreed to join a few friends on a fishing trip for an entire week. *He won't even know I'm gone*, Mae thought.

It was a two-hour drive from the Ozarks to Kansas City, plus another thirty minutes to KCI. Mae made plans to sleep at Dominique's loft apartment in order to catch the noon flight on Tuesday to Lynchburg, Virginia. The plan was Dominique would drop her off at the airport, and then double back to the Ozarks to house-sit, while Mae's husband, John, was on his fishing trip.

THE ROGUE RIVER
GRANTS PASS, OR
MONDAY NIGHT

The men enjoyed one day of world-class fishing, when Bud busted down the aisle at the diner that evening. "Hey guys, heads up. Got a call from my daughter and my granddaughter is sick. I need to be home. The guide will refund our money, and we can come back, or you can stay if you want, but I've got to go."

All three men agreed it was more important to fly Bud back to the Ozarks.

KANSAS CITY INTERNATIONAL AIRPORT
KANSAS CITY, MO
TUESDAY 9:00AM

"I'm sick," Mae said as Dominique's 1992 red and gray Mustang wove in and out of airport traffic.

"We're early enough to grab breakfast. I told you to cut back on the caffeine," replied Dominique.

Mae hadn't been in an airport for decades; much had changed. "I hate to fly," said Mae.

"Aw, come on, you were complaining the other day you felt, I believe the word you used was, smothered," retorted Dominique.

"Yeah, this is going to be good. On the other hand, I'm beginning to feel guilty I didn't tell John. Feels dishonest," said Mae.

"Just think how much he keeps from you, you know, so he won't be called hen pecked," Dominique added. Both women giggled.

"Poor guy," said Mae conspiratorially.

"Poor guy my ass!" replied Dominique.

NEW LONDON AIRPORT
LYNCHBURG, VA
TUESDAY 3:00PM

"Hello! Over here!" called out Connie Bryan towards the attractive brunette in the red Chanel suit coming towards her. "Wow!" said Connie. "Not the usual church secretary look. I don't know what I was expecting, but your appearance surprises me."

"Oh? Am I overdressed or underdressed?" Mae said, alarmed.

"Well, it's just, well, I think Dr. Peterson was expecting a little old lady with a steno pad, not a fashion model with a laptop," clarified Connie. "Any luggage?"

"No," answered Mae. "I have what I need right here." She patted her two carry-on bags.

With the airport ticket patrol closing in behind them, Connie Bryan and Mae Lancaster zipped out of the loading zone, and merged onto the ramp toward Highway 29 in Connie's dark blue Trailblazer. After they exchanged hellos, Dr. Warren Peterson's trusted assistant began to update Mae on her itinerary.

"I'm going to settle you in at the hotel we talked about—then tomorrow I'll send a car about 9:00 am. Dr. Peterson will meet you at the offices on the north end of the complex around 10:00 am. He may or may not be able to have lunch with us, but never mind, you'll have your presentation given, and that's the main thing," Connie directed.

"I don't know how to thank you for arranging this interview," Mae said with humility.

"Both Dr. Peterson and I are curious as to what your survey is about, Mrs. Lancaster," Connie whispered.

"Oh, please call me Mae." Bracing herself, Mae Lancaster bravely continued. "I didn't say anything on purpose because it is such a passionate subject, but my survey questions to five thousand women are about keeping family planning, birth control, and women's health out of politics."

"Oh my!" exclaimed Connie. "That IS going to give Warren a run for his money," Connie chuckled.

"Well, I thought the largest Christian publisher should know what women thought about the issue. Que Sera Sera."

Both women became quiet. *As if I don't have enough on my mind,* Connie thought.

ANOTHER CORRUPT GOVERNOR
MADISON, WI

Governor Steven Haggard was under investigation for what was defined as *Patronage*, the hiring of his own supporters for many open government jobs, some of whom had been found incompetent. When the indictment came down, there was also evidence of paid favors.

****

ANOTHER CORRUPT SENATOR

Senator Eli Cook was proud of his new glossy mailer that would arrive in every Wisconsin home today, claiming to support seniors and workers. In truth, he had been working hard to stop the new benefit programs, with the payoff being acceptance into, and recognition by Wisconsin's elite upper crust.

UNION JUSTICE
MADISON, WI

Iron Worker Representative Drayton Morris sat in the union office attempting to prepare for the upcoming negotiations with the Governor of Wisconsin, knowing it was hopeless. "Are you sure you don't want to see what you can do to help our workers, Governor?" the union man asked, staring off into space questioning the imaginary governor. Heavy at heart and discouraged, Drayton Morris folded up his hopes and desires for the working class of Wisconsin, and went home.

The Letter

It was that same evening Drayton received two pieces of mail. The deceptive political advertisement from the senator from Wisconsin, "Clever, very clever," he said, tossing the fraudulent mailer into a nearby trashcan. And *a letter*.

He understood the instructions on *the letter* he received. *What's it to me?* His doctor had diagnosed Alzheimer's. What was going to happen to him? First, the simple misspelling of words, then spoons put in the fork drawer, and then keys wouldn't fit into the lock. Because he was not going to know *anyone* or *anything* in the very near future, Drayton Morris, union man, began to make plans. First on the agenda was to rent a limousine.

TIMMS HILL, WISCONSIN (1,951 feet, the highest point in Wisconsin)
ON A MONDAY

"I'm late! I'm late!" screamed the governor to his driver.

Governor Steven Haggard's limousine driver was not his customary chauffeur. Angry, the annoyed governor noticed the scenery wasn't familiar. "Excuse me, sir, excuse me. Where ARE we going?"

****

TIMMS HILL, WISCONSIN (1,951 feet, the highest point in Wisconsin)
ON TUESDAY

"I'm late! I'm late!" screamed Senator Eli Cook to his driver. The Senator's limousine driver also was not his customary chauffeur.

A BLACKOUT
ETERNAL HOUSE OF PUBLISHING
COMPLEX
TUESDAY EVENING

It had been over a week since Dr. Stan Anders walked out of the publishing complex, leaving Warren Peterson baffled. Stan's reports and another review of the disk continued to not make sense.

There have not been any new author contracts from the locations Stan traveled to, Warren thought. He had checked. What could his friend have been doing in California, Florida, or at the race-track in Lexington, Kentucky? There was something else bothering him. *What was it?* Warren concentrated. *Oh, yes, Stan denied being seen with that Middle Eastern gentleman, when I saw him in Atlanta.* He murmured, "Hmmm, perhaps that's a clue."

Warren slipped the disk into his coat pocket, and headed over to turn out the lights. He was startled when a man's silhouette appeared in the doorway, blocking it. Flipping the lights back on, Warren said, "What brings you to lurk around the offices, Stan?

"Uh, I forgot. I want to take my father's book-case with me." Anders threw out the answer to see if it would stick.

"Stan, I am glad to see you, I've been worried about you. I'll help you with the bookcase."

A pickpocket couldn't have done a smoother job of slipping the disk from his coat pocket to the coffee table, and shuffle magazines to hide it.

Footsteps echoed as they walked in silence through the corridors with the hustle of the day long gone. When they crossed in front of the groundskeeper's office, Warren noticed the lights still on. Leaning into the threshold, he called, "Hello, Mrs. Hana? Are you working late this evening?"

Then everything went black.

LYNCHBURG MARRIOTT
TUESDAY NIGHT

Mae looked around her room. *There is nothing like being able to close the door of your hotel room, lock it with the dead bolt, kick your shoes off and sit on the bed and relax a minute.* "I love it!" she exclaimed. "A little independence feels great."

She decided not to call Dominique, since the trip was one night, and there wasn't a cell phone signal where her husband was fishing. As far as she could tell, there were no loose ends; she was all on her own.

Mae put on her night clothes, and switched back and forth from prime time news to the History Channel, and began to think about her husband. *Life isn't going too well for us now, is it, honey?* she thought, *I'm sorry I'm not who you wanted me to be.*

Mae continued to analyze. *With the time difference, it's 7:00 pm at home in the Ozarks. Dominique's there with the animals.*

The hotel window looked out over unfamiliar surroundings, and Mae's mind drifted to the meeting tomorrow with the Christian publisher. *What am I doing here? What in the world do I hope to accomplish?*

With her confidence fading, she always found solace with 70% cocoa dark chocolate, the big bar, and the SyFy channel.

A WHITE HOUSE UPDATE

Some did not want an unprecedented female President, and although there were many well-wishers on Inauguration Day, it had been a real fight to earn respect. It had been much easier to work with the generals as Commander-in-Chief than with many on both sides of the aisle, whose resentment toward her was also unprecedented. Much to the dismay of President Adams' enemies, she signed several bills into law helping the American people. She worked for the people, did not expect the people to work for her, and the people loved her for it. But President Saundra Adams wasn't concerned about re-election now. She was determined to catch a conspirator. The murders made no sense but did have a common denominator. All victims were from the Legislative and Judicial branches of government, so far.

"Do we have any news from NSA, Madam President?" asked Secret Service Agent Wiley. The agent could tell by looking the answer was an emphatic NO, nevertheless the President replied anyway.

"Every judge, Senator and House member has doubled their security, and are looking over their shoulders," said the President. "If this ordeal wasn't so terrifying, it would be comical. The most powerful men and women in America are accustomed to others jumping at their command, but not today, no, not today. There is a real separating of the men and the boys going on. How's the media?"

"In frenzy, I hear," reported Agent Wiley.

****

Many Americans wanted certain politicians D-E-A-D. Now THEY WERE turning up D-E-A-D. A real crisis was upon the President, and the United States of America.

NO SHOW AND STAND DOWN
ETERNAL HOUSE OF PUBLISHING
WEDNESDAY 1:00PM

Mae had been sitting alone in Dr. Warren Peterson's executive office for hours. *Well, let's see, I've gone over my presentation twice, rehearsed what I am going to say to my husband, who doesn't know I'm here, and read all the magazines piled high on this coffee table!* Mae found herself stacking and organizing magazines. *What a messy coffee table. It doesn't go with the rest of this office!* Annoyed she stood to stretch. *And now my stomach is going to growl in my meeting because I skipped breakfast.*

Meanwhile, Connie had been attempting to reach Warren. *Warren is always on time and expects punctuality in others,* thought Connie. His car was in his space. She had been all over the large complex, and checked with department heads.

Connie stuck her head into Warren's office. "Well, I guess I'll have to call *MRS*. Peterson."

Mae couldn't help catching the horrified look on Connie's face at the prospect of calling Dr. Warren Peterson's wife. "Is she hard to get along with?" Mae inquired.

"No," Connie answered. "It's just Julie Peterson and I have known each other a long time. We stay out of each other's way. Now I have to call her."

A few minutes later, Connie again stuck her head into Warren's office. "Mrs. Peterson's not home. I left a message."

✳✳✳✳✳✳✳✳✳✳✳✳

Several hours later, with no Dr. Warren Peterson, she made a decision. "Well, grab your stuff, Mae. I'm so sorry. I'll order up sandwiches from the cafeteria. Have you checked out of the hotel?" Connie tried to manage the botched day.

"Yes, I have everything with me," said Mae, as she gathered her laptop and notes. It was all she could do to bite back the tears of disappointment. She mustn't let this woman see her act unprofessionally. *It isn't Connie's fault the dirtbag didn't show.* Mae's drooping shoulders told it all. She had a plane to catch, and didn't dare spend another day without John knowing where she was.

Before they could leave the office, the switchboard lit up with a buzz. Connie and Mae jumped in unison. Over the speakerphone both women could hear Julie Peterson's angry tone. "No, I haven't seen Warren since yesterday. And when you see him, tell him I'm at my mother's."

Connie's apologies on the way to the airport were sincere; nevertheless, she was anxious to get rid of the church secretary from Missouri, so the real search for Dr. Warren Peterson could begin.

OIL THAT IS, TEXAS GOLD
SAN ANTONIO, TX

ALLClear Drilling Corporation was recognized as one of the safest and capable drilling services to gas and oil in the world. At the top of their game, their common stock traded on the NYSE under the symbol ADC.

New to the top one percent of the wealthy, oil tycoon David Dunning, the majority stockholder of ADC, had worked his way up, starting as a pump operator in his twenties, a mast hand in his thirties, an OIM responsible for essential platform decisions in his forties; now a powerful CEO.

David Dunning first met corrupt Texas judge Isaiah Oakley from Austin at a Corpus Christie society meeting supporting the oil industry. The two began to meet over dinner to manage big money for the non-profit Oil Drilling Historical Museum.

The Letter

Forged documents were often used to conceal other thefts. Documents claiming money had been borrowed but in reality had been stolen were sometimes hard to find in an audit. David Dunning and Judge Isaiah Oakley had been cooking the books of the Oil and Gas Historical Society for years. When a theft involved public money taken by a supposedly responsible public official, like a judge, it became political.

The day Dunning received *his letter* happened to be the same day he discovered the FBI snooping around the judge's two sets of books. *I have worked my whole life to get where I am. How could I have been so greedy to jeopardize my company?* He scrutinized *the letter* he received in the mail. *I don't believe in coincidence. This letter is the answer. I must eliminate the trail. I have no other choice.*

****

The dark van came out of nowhere and swerved onto the jogger path, knocking him to the ground. "Someone tried to kill me," the judge cried out. "Bastards! I saw your license plate!" I'll get YOU," he continued to boast as the van's taillights disappeared.

The coolness of the ground began to seep under his clothes. Judge Isaiah Oakley lifted himself up on one elbow. Before the judge could recall his list of enemies, he identified the roar of the returning van ...*thump, bump...* the last thing his ears ever heard.

THE SEARCH
ETERNAL HOUSE OF PUBLISHING
COMPLEX
WEDNESDAY LATE

Connie searched for Warren room to room and corridor to corridor, as nonchalant as possible.

She, too, had noticed a change in Dr. Stan Anders. Although she did not know him as well as Warren did, Connie heard through the cafeteria gossip that Stan's wife had left, and no one had seen him around the complex.

I never did think much of his capabilities; not sorry to see him go. She thought about Stan. *Always been more of a crazy academic than a business man...and that wandering eye doesn't help. Connie, stop! That's unkind.*

Connie leaned against the groundskeeper's desk and chastised herself for her judgmental attitude. "Oh, my aching feet." She sat down to contemplate where to search next, and then heard something.

What was that? A groan?

WEDNESDAY LATE AT KCI

The first thing Mae noticed as she came down the plane's unloading ramp was her friend Dominique's troubled expression and body language. Her friend's usually perfect hair was sticking out from her headband, and her clothes didn't match. "You look like you've been on an all-night binge, said Mae.

"So do you," said Dominique.

"It was a waste of time," answered Mae. "A great big nothing; didn't even see the guy. He stood me up, and his poor secretary had to cover for him. I don't care. I'm through with this one-woman campaign against 'the Beast,'" said Mae. "All I care about now is getting home before John."

"You're going to hate what I have to tell you," began Domi. "John came home yesterday. Bud's granddaughter's sick and John caught me house-sitting. I had to tell him where you were, Mae. I had to. No lie would come to my lips with him standing there staring a hole in me," said Dominique, exasperated.

"Oh, my God!" Mae's heart sank. She was in the doghouse.

GROUNDSKEEPER'S OFFICE
ETERNAL HOUSE OF PUBLISHING
COMPLEX

The sound of the groans brought Connie leaning against a locked door at the back of the groundskeeper's office. "Hello? Anybody in there?" she whispered.

"Connie! It's me, Warren, I'm hurt!"

"What are you doing in there, Warren?" Connie asked, not that she wanted to know.

"The key to this supply room is on Mrs. Hana's master ring. No one is supposed to know, but everyone knows she keeps them hanging in her medicine cabinet."

Warren fell through the doorway into Connie's arms as the door opened.

"No, no I didn't see a thing, hit from behind." Warren gave Connie a summary of the past twenty-four hours, as she examined the knot on the back of his head.

"Connie, Stan Anders is in some kind of trouble," he continued his story. "He attacked me," Warren said, with an unbelieving whimper. "Quick! Back to my office, I left the disk there!"

Bewildered, Connie asked, "What disk?"

"The computer disk I should have told you about when you asked the first time." He held her gaze until she looked down at his wrinkled suit, then back up again, to his disheveled hair, and fatigued face.

****

"No disk!" Warren doubled over in defeat. "He has it!"

Connie said, "No Warren. Mae Lancaster, who you were supposed to meet with, probably picked it up by mistake, since she had her presentation sitting on top of this same stack of magazines. We were hurrying to make her flight."

Warren kept a pack of cigarettes in the bottom of his desk drawer, although he had quit the habit years ago. All he wanted to do was fill his lungs of the long ago missed aroma.

"Want a cigarette?"

"Sure, why not."

Warren watched his secretary take an unsuccessful drag and smash the cigarette in his silver-plated ashtray only for looks.

BACK HOME IN THE OZARKS

"Honey, don't sweat it," John said to his wife. "I'm sorry the meeting didn't go the way you wanted it to," he continued. "I'm not mad, but what if something happened?" He sounded concerned.

A dinner and a movie almost always made amends for Mae and John Lancaster. A few days later the episode was in the past, or so she thought.

****

"That tour to Israel you wanted to go on is leaving next week. You still have time to sign up. You have your passport." John said, making a rare appearance in Mae's laundry room.

Surprised and somewhat alarmed, Mae asked, "Why now?"

"You've wanted to go for years!" He continued the pitch. "I'll feed the animals."

"Don't you want to go with me?" Mae's voice was high and pleading.

"No!" said John.

Mae continued to fold clothes, and felt entirely alone.

SOMETHING'S WRONG, BUT WHAT

It would take Warren Peterson and Connie Bryan some time to unwind and regroup. Almost a whole week went by without a word from Dr. Stan Anders. They had both tried to put the whole matter about the computer disk out of their minds, and go about their work as usual. But Warren was unable to.

"Connie, I need to do something about Stan. Will you contact Mae Lancaster and see if she wants to reschedule; and see if you can retrieve that disk?"

"Yes, I was thinking the same thing."

Relieved, Warren added, "Good. I'll go to Atlanta and visit Stan's apartment."

SANTA CATALINA ISLAND LANDING
HUNTINGTON BEACH, CA

He thought he had covered his tracks, yet someone had seen him in Nogales. Twenty-five to life didn't fit into Glenn E. Colton's plan; he had to leave the country.

The news media had begun to report the deaths of U.S. Congressmen, but as yet, could not connect the dots. Colton wondered how many were involved in the conspiracy. Perhaps the FBI should be informed. He wasn't sorry for his part; he eliminated a treasonous thief and a murderer. Nevertheless, *What if someone isn't guilty and gets caught in the trap?* He was beginning to see the fallacy of the plan. It was time to say goodbye to Santa Maria, and the life he had shared with Ann.

Colton's subconscious took over. Before he knew it, his most treasured items were packed, items given to friends, and mounds of trash sacks stacked for pickup. *Homes and bodies are shells we're passing through,* he reckoned.

His long-time friend from Long Beach was waiting on the forty-two foot Hallberg-Rassy Swedish sailing ocean cruiser the two had invested in together.

These old friends sailed Catalina more times than they could count, and together had over 200,000 ocean miles, and twenty-five years of sailing experience. Each could handle the boat in case of illness or seasickness. The boat was equipped with a powerful autopilot, a dependable wind-vane self-steering system, and electric winches had been installed to aid a man with leg braces. Their beautiful boat, *The Madam DuBarry*, was built to carry the additional weight of anchors, chains, drinking water, fuel, life raft, dinghy and outboard. There was one more thing to do.

He hired a taxi to deliver his envelope to the FBI. It contained *the letter* he had received, and a brief explanation as to why he had done what he had done. The thought of never returning to America was no longer important. Retired U.S. Army Special Forces Glenn E. Colton had done his part to keep her free, twice.

J. EDGAR HOOVER BUILDING
WASHINGTON, DC

Director of the FBI Conway had been pacing, as usual. *The string of deaths looks like the work of an assassin...*pace, pace...*or could be more than one assassin...*pace, pace.

FBI Agent Jeanes buzzed herself in unannounced. "We have a break in the case, sir."

The Director took his desk, and motioned the agent to make her report.

"The California Field Office has been working on the Senator McDaniel car shooting, one to the forehead. They received an envelope containing what appears to be a confession, and a copy of the conspiracy *letter* we are working on from Turkey. Sir, the SAME LETTER we received from TURKEY!"

Excited, the Director stood. "What's the connection?"

"So far the investigation indicates the manila envelope arrived, alone, by taxi courier. It is from a retired U.S. Army man, Special Forces Glenn E. Colton, Viet Nam injury, leg braces for life. His file reflects honorable discharge, medaled, widower, and mobile, considering his injury; makes big money in food imports."

"Where is Colton now, Agent Jeanes?" inquired the Director.

"Gone." Embarrassed, the agent continued. "He has been gone a few days according to his co-workers. His house is locked up tight; may have been emptied of mementos. That's not all, sir. Colton may be connected to the dead gun-runner in Arizona. A crippled man was identified at the scene."

The Director resumed his pacing. "There's a connection between the Senator and the gun-runner. Find it!"

FBI
CLARKSBURG, WV

FBI Agent Cherie Leigh's expertise in handwriting analysis landed her in Clarksburg, West Virginia where ninety-six million sets of fingerprints from across the United States were stored. Agent Leigh prepared three reports for profiling:

Report 1: *The letter* received from the Republic of Turkey contained three sets of prints: the criminal detained in Istanbul carrying *the letter;* Sarp Asker, known terrorist from the Province of Izmir, not Al Qaeda. Third prints are of Dr. Stan Anders, Doctor of Ministry, Lynchburg, Virginia, no subversive history.

Report 2: The forged loan application which turned up at the Bank of Corpus Christie have the prints of deceased hit and run victim, Texas judge Isaiah Oakley;

Report 3: The prints on the picture of the adolescent female found in the Florida Governor's cabin in Apalachicola are those of Barbara Jones, age thirty-seven; resides in Boca Raton, Florida, owns a retail store; prints from a conceal and carry weapon's course.

Discreet inquiries are being made.

KCI TO LAGUARDIA
SUNDAY

"I haven't flown in fifteen years; now two flights in two weeks. This one transatlantic!" said Mae. "I've always wanted to see Galilee, but now I am going, is it a good idea?" Mae continued to complain.

"There you go again. You're all set. This is just what you need. Why aren't you excited?" questioned Dominique. "What is all that stuff you are bringing, anyway?" Domi pointed and disapproved of Mae's laptop and the backpack she carried her binders in.

"I think he wants me out of the way. I think he may be seeing another woman," confided Mae in a sickened whisper.

"Who could it be?" demanded Dominique.

"Someone more like himself, I suppose. In answer to your question, I'm bringing my laptop because there may be downtime on the tour buses."

Worried, Dominique watched her friend disappear into the terminal, and put her Mustang in gear.

BEN GURION INTERNATIONAL AIRPORT
TEL AVIV, ISRAEL
TUESDAY MORNING

Since Mae Lancaster registered late for the Israel tour, she missed the Sunday flight everyone else was on. Her Monday Delta Flight connection through New York went smoothly, and she was now standing in the world famous Israeli airport. The Ben Gurion was operated by the Israel Airports Authority, a government-owned corporation managing all public airports and border crossings. They, of course, took security serious. Airport security guards operated both in uniform, and undercover. Mae could not help taking in everything she could to see if she could identify any spies!

"Mrs. Lancaster, Mrs. Lancaster, over here." Their attention caught, several turned their heads, and Mae was one of them.

"Here! Here!" Mae yelled, afraid she would miss her transportation.

Travel agent, Lisa Cohen, had been notified there would be one more guest joining her tour. She noticed right away this late-comer knew a lot about Israel. She would not have to repeat her entire welcome-to-Israel spiel. The new arrival was, however, curious about security.

"The IAA has been planning a major upgrade of our baggage screening," recited the travel agent. "Did you know all checked baggage is put in a pressure chamber to trigger any possible explosives?"

"Good," said Mae, well aware of the situation Israel was in with her neighbors.

Lisa and Mae enjoyed a delightful conversation on the ride to a wonderful three-star hotel minutes from the beach.

THE GRAND BEACH HOTEL
TEL AVIV
TUESDAY EVENING

Mae swallowed hard, taking in her beautiful room with an excellent view of Tel Aviv. At $126 per night, it wasn't the most or least expensive; Lisa Cohen Travel Agency had used them for years because her guests were treated wonderfully.

I'm glad I paid extra to not have a roommate. Mae sighed with relief. *John was a dear not to have squawked, after all, there were no other roommates because of the late sign-in. Halleluiah!* Mae opened her laptop, spreading her journals and binders onto the second full-size bed.

She settled into the hotel room that was going to be her home for the next ten days, and then dropped onto the bed, clothes and all, and passed right out.

LEXINGTON POLICE DEPARTMENT
LEXINGTON, KY

"Hey, Sergeant, you'll never believe what kind of call I took today," said the police detective. "As if we don't have enough to do, now we're the pet patrol," the detective added.

The police sergeant hated working the night desk. His double-take at the red-faced detective turned into a triple-take. "What do we have here?"

A cat carrier case with two angry green eyes peering out was in one hand, and in the other hand was a leash, with a dog on it, a chocolate poodle with an attitude.

"The Day Desk took a call they didn't know what to do with, and passed it to me," continued the detective. "The animal shelter picked up this Persian cat and Standard Poodle with microchips belonging to that murdered Supreme Court judge. There is a FBI Bulletin if any station stumbles on to anything to do with the judge, we're to call it in."

"Oh, for goodness' sakes, the FBI must be DESPARATE!" said the disbelieving sergeant.

"Yeah, maybe the cat and the Poodle will crack the case!" the detective added.

The sergeant and the detective could not stop laughing.

J. EDGAR HOOVER BUILDING
WASHINGTON, DC

FBI Agent Jeanes could not believe her luck; two leads in two days.

"Director Conway, we have a known arsonist in custody in Lexington, Kentucky wanting to plea bargain — wants to give up the guy, he says, ordered the hit on Justice Hopkins.

"Who is he, who ordered the hit?" The FBI Director drew a sign of relief. Maybe the case was getting somewhere.

"A guy under investigation by the Kentucky Horse Racing people, GAMBLING implications," the Agent clarified.

"Agent Jeanes…," began the Director.

"I know, I know, get your plane readied," answered the agent.

ETERNAL HOUSE OF PUBLISHING OFFICES

The executive floor offices didn't feel the same. *It's time to leave this job, leave Warren. Yes, I am going to resign when this is over. The role of the other woman was never, well, I deserve better. It is going to be up to me to bring closure to these relationships.*

The nightmare with Stan Anders brought anxiety to the surface, and Connie felt depression and exhaustion rush over her. She had been trying to call the Lancaster house for days, with no answer.

Connie was also thinking about Mae. When Connie told Mae about her grown daughter in California, Mae had said "California! Oh, my! She needs to move inland, don't you know California is going to drop into the ocean, could be anytime!" They had laughed, and each confessed they had stocked pantries. She admired Mae for the new ideas she wanted to accomplish. However, big changes in thinking came hard, and slowly, if at all.

Connie took a breath and continued to hit re-dial. She needed to find the woman she never thought she would see again, and locate the computer disk.

BACK AT THE LANCASTERS

"Too bad the fishing trip was screwed," Bud Kennedy yelled over a rooftop. Several of the Timbers Cross locals had gathered to help a neighbor put a roof on his new metal building. Several men were on ladders, two on the roof, and a rover carried materials.

"No big deal, Bud, I shouldn't have left home anyway, Mae and I've been…distant. I've been a jerk, don't know why," John said. "That's why I paid for the trip she's on, thought it might get me off the hook," he added. "This trip is costing me five grand!"

The crew headed over to the marina to wind down, but John didn't go. He wanted to be home by the phone, and it was indeed ringing as he walked in.

THE PHONE CALLS BEGIN

Mae's husband answered. "Yes, this is John Lancaster."

"Mr. Lancaster, this is Connie Bryan at the Eternal House of Publishing in Lynchburg. I was wondering if I could speak with your lovely wife, Mae."

Always on guard, John inquired, "Who is this again?"

"Ms. Bryan, from the publishing company, Connie Bryan," she repeated. "I enjoyed meeting your wife, and wanted to apologize again for the misunderstanding on her visit. Dr. Peterson was terribly sorry. He had been detained with car trouble outside of a phone signal." Connie used her professional, courteous voice, and was quite surprised how easy it was to lie.

"You could speak to her if she was here. I put her on a plane several days ago for a ten-day tour to Israel. She's out of reach." John wanted to imply there was no sense in trying.

"Oh, no, I MUST speak with her. Mr. Lancaster, she accidentally picked up a computer disk of Dr. Peterson's. We need to see if she can locate it." Connie bit her lip wondering if the words had come out right.

"A computer what?" John hated to talk on the phone, and this conversation was getting too much for his taste. "Ms. Bryan, all I can do is take a message."

"May I have the number of her travel agency, please?" Connie sounded desperate.

"Uhhh, I don't think so." John started to feel pressured.

"Please, Mr. Lancaster, this disk is important."

John began to comprehend this woman was in trouble, and she needed Mae. He concentrated. *What to do, what to do....* "Okay, Ms. Bryan, you won't need to call the travel agency. I'll give you Mae's cell phone number."

****

John Lancaster grilled himself a steak, and found the left over baked beans and coleslaw. The evening news didn't interest him, neither did basketball.

ISRAEL
CAESAREA, MT. CARMEL, MEGIDDO,
NAZARETH
WEDNESDAY, DAY 1 OF TOUR

All set with her camera, best walking shoes, and a light jacket, Mae met the others in her group and took her place on the bus. Again, she was glad she didn't have a roommate, *unless it could have been John, of course.*

The Mediterranean coastline was beautiful, but without her husband to share it, the trip was missing something. *He would have loved it*, Mae imagined. *But, you can't tell HIM anything! I wonder what he is doing. Is he missing me?*

In Caesarea they saw where Cornelius was baptized. Then they were at the top of Mt. Carmel, where Elijah prayed and defeated the prophets of Baal. The Valley of Megiddo held special interest as Mae visualized a worldwide battle, and Nazareth, Nazareth, its name sent chills up her arms.

The day went fine, lots of information, lots of pictures. The ancient streets were enough to feel close to God.

Back at her hotel, Mae chose to eat in her room, rest, and fuss with her journals. Buried deep in her backpack was the computer disk the whole world was searching for, and she was unaware of the danger.

ISRAEL
SEA OF GALILEE, CAPERNAUM
THURSDAY, DAY 2 OF TOUR

After a wonderful Israeli buffet breakfast, Mae's tour group took a boat ride around the Sea of Galilee, and visited the Horns of Hattin where some say Jesus gave the Sermon on the Mount. *Oh, what a wonderful world if we could follow His instructions.* Mae thought. *Is mankind EVER going to get it?*

From Mae's incredible vantage point she could see the ruins of an ancient church. "On this slope of the mountain there is said to be a holy site called in Arabic, 'Nebi Shu'ayb', the tomb of the prophet Jethro, the father–in-law of Moses." Mae listened to Lisa in the background. "Archaeological excavations have revealed a large synagogue dating to the Byzantine period on the summit," Lisa continued.

At day's end, the exhausted tourists climbed back on the bus to return to their private affairs.

DISCOVERED
BOCA RATON, FL

The FBI stood in Barbara's living room. "Can you identify this photograph, Ms. Jones?"

A picture of her daughter, Randie, stared up from the FBI agent's hand. Barbara recognized the pose she had framed for her brother, Harry.

"Yes, this is a picture of my daughter." Her hand wanted to shake, but she managed to fake calmness. "I give this picture all over the place," she said, as matter-of-fact. "I'm proud of her, you know. Randie is going to the state swimming finals."

The agent remained unmoved by the friendly chit-chat. "This photo was found where Governor Scott Randall was last seen, Ms. Jones. This is serious business. Care to think again?" he responded, cold and arrogant.

Barbara answered evenly and as cool, "I can't imagine why this picture was found there. Maybe the Governor has friends on the state swimming finals, also."

"Where is the child's father, Ms. Jones?" The second FBI Agent broke into the verbal duel with a feeble attempt to play the good cop, to the routine.

"Randie's father has been missing since the day she was born. We have nothing to do with EITHER of your missing men. I feel quite certain you will find the same. Good day, gentlemen."

Barbara didn't breathe until the car with the government license backed out of her driveway, and disappeared out of sight.

****

"Mr. Link?" said Barbara. "There are roaches in my living room. After you receive this message, call me at the hardware store." Barbara and Harry Walden shared a code since they were children. If Barbara, or Randie, were in trouble, Mr. Link meant "needing rescue," roaches were the police, and the hardware store owned by a close friend in Boca, was the one next to the Dairy Queen.

FBI ONE STEP AHEAD

"Why didn't you tell her about the second set of prints belonging to her brother?" said the short one.

"Because we're listening in; she'll meet him. The photo came out of a frame," said the tall one.

"You know she's clean, don't you?"

"Yes, but there is a connection; care to make a stab at it?"

"You've solved the case?"

"Yep! The kid looks like the Governor. Same face."

THE GRAND BEACH HOTEL
TEL AVIV
FRIDAY, DAY 3 OF TOUR

Let's see, what shall I do today? Mae meditated on brochures, and scrutinized her maps spread across the bed. What Lisa described as the group's free day came as a welcome relief to Mae, itching to get off by herself.

Some were going to the Holocaust Archives, but Mae decided against joining them. *Israel is always close to peril,* she acknowledged. *The Jews won't be marching into ovens any time soon, without taking as many of their enemies with them,* Mae asserted. *I wonder why the Jews were chosen to play their peculiar part in the human drama.* As she asked the question, she answered it herself. *Was it because they were the least in number? Hummm, God often uses the small in a big way.* Mae decided this reason had merit.

Here's something of interest, Nehemiah's Wall archaeological site. Artifacts had been found under a tower from the fifth century B.C., the time of Nehemiah. *Hummm, and many scholars have argued the wall didn't exist...if stones could speak.*

Mae continued reading until the ring tone from her cell phone registered in her brain. *Where's the cell phone? Who could it be? John? Could something be wrong?*

"Hello, this is Mae Lancaster," she answered, timidly. "CONNIE!" Mae was glad to hear a familiar voice.

Mae planned to give top priority to Connie Bryan's request to find the missing disk when she got back from the days tour.

THE GRAND BEACH HOTEL
TEL AVIV
FRIDAY LATE AFTERNOON

Dr. Warren Peterson's secretary had been urgent and frank. *Now what did she say again?* It wasn't what Connie had said, it was how she said it. Mae was to guard the disk with her life.

Was she kidding? She sure didn't sound like she was kidding.

"If I have the missing disk, it is in my dead file," Mae determined. She didn't want to think about that horrible publisher meeting.

She began to analyze. *John isn't going to want to go into my office, and look for something he doesn't know what he is looking for. And besides, do I really want him snooping?*

She would call Dominique. Domi could get in, and get out, and mail the disk straight to Connie Bryan.

After several hours of telephone tag, Mae pleaded with her friend. "Well, can you do it? Can you do it, Domi?"

"Sure, sounds intriguing! It will take me a few hours. I'll watch for John, and find your disk," Dominique assured Mae.

"Let me give you the address to overnight it. Be sure and use one of those bubble wrap envelopes. Will you call me when it's done?"

"Yes, yes, and yes, no problemo!"

****

Mae wanted to resume her vacation. The following day's tour was going to be a long one, beginning at the Pool of Siloam where the blind man received sight, and ending at Pilate's Judgment Hall in the Fortress of Antonia.

That evening Mae mingled, and chatted with a few of her new friends, but was anxious to return to the solitude of her hotel room.

BACK IN THE OZARKS
EARLY SATURDAY MORNING

A frustrated Dominique followed Mae's instructions to the letter. No disk. "Where is that blanketey blank disk?" She looked everywhere, under desks, over bookcases, in between equipment.

"How am I supposed to find a disk around here?" Dominique's hands were flying. Mae had specifically told Dominique the disk would not be mixed in with her own computer supplies.

"Hi, Dominique," said John as he leaned lackadaisically in the doorway, studying her.

Startled, she cried, "Oh, hi, John, well therrrrre you arrrrre!" Dominique, for the second time, found herself face-to-face with her best friend's husband. She stuttered, and stammered as if she had been caught robbing a bank.

John listened to yet another of his wife and her friend's yarns.

DR. STAN ANDERS' APARTMENT
ATLANTA
SATURDAY MORNING

"I want out," demanded Stan to his Turkish overseer. "I'm through."

"How regrettable, Meester Anders. We do not work that way. You know too much about our business to walk away. Sarp Asker would assume trust had been broken."

Stan could not see the eyes of the dark man in sunglasses. "I didn't mean to infer I will be any trouble. I'll return to Istanbul myself," Stan added.

"You do that." The sly foreigner smelled of fish and garlic. "One last question, who did you say had the names, and addresses of our assassins?"

"No one, it's been lost, misplaced, someone walked out with it, and doesn't know what it is. It will not be a problem to us."

The world crashed in as Dr. Stan Anders tried to make light of the events that had spun out of control.

"Oh, really?" the imposing man said, but it was not a question.

THE GRAND BEACH HOTEL
TEL AVIV
SATURDAY MORNING, DAY 4 OF TOUR

The lamp table next to the wide picture window in Mae's hotel room was the perfect place to wait to meet for tours. She could gaze out at the city and enjoy every minute. The Tower of David was one of Jerusalem's most sacred sites, tucked inside the walls of the Old City, now a museum. Visitors could walk back two thousand years, peek into ancient cisterns, and walk in the shadow of Crusader arches. She had two hours to wait for the tour, and hoped Dominique's phone call would come before she had to leave.

As Mae secured her cell phone onto her belt, the ring tone came through nice and clear.

"I can't find the disk and was caught again," said a peeved Dominique.

"What? Why do I trust you when you say no problemo?" Mae teased.

"It's not a laughing matter, Mae, John didn't act mad, but moody," Domi reported.

"I can't imagine where that darn thing can be," said Mae, trying to think.

"Do YOU have it?" Dominique pressed. "You left with your backpack, ya know."

Mae hesitated. "Well, you may be right; I did transfer some things from my laptop to my backpack. After a few long minutes, a sheepish Mae said, "I guess I do have it."

"Oh, for goodness' sakes, Mae! I'm going to kill you! I drove two hours, and had to deal with John, and you had it all the time? You'll pay for this one, Mae."

****

Mae Lancaster slipped the mysterious CD into her laptop drive, and up popped a mailing list. Names and addresses in different cities; a *Mail Merge document. Humph, doesn't look like a life or death situation to me,* Mae thought, a little on the disappointed side.

****

Mae was going to be late to the King David Royal Palace, and she began to hurry.

The tour would take forty-five minutes, and she planned to return to the hotel lobby, and ask for assistance to express mail a package.

She locked her hotel room, and made haste to the elevator where she resorted to counting flowers in the carpet, and waited for the sluggish elevator doors to open. When the doors slid to the side, a formidable man dressed in black, wearing sunglasses, started to get off, but hesitated to wait for Mae to get on. Mae did not get on. They stared at each other, frozen in time.

Mae was thinking, *Go back for the CD*. She had considered taking it with her, but had decided against it. Now, she was going to have to go back, and lose precious time.

Mae explained to the man on the elevator, "I forgot my phone. I'll catch the next one."

Although she could not see his eyes, Mae saw the man's head turn downward at her cell phone attached to her belt, as the elevator doors closed. "That was weird," said Mae. "What just happened there?"

In a trance, Mae doubled back to her room, and tossed the CD into her shoulder bag. *Was that a premonition?* She wondered.

With a shrug, Mae decided this would be her best chance to use the restroom. *I must have a bladder the size of a pea!* As she tugged at her jeans, *Kerplunk!* Mae's cell phone splashed down into the bowl. Horrified, Mae yelled, "Oh, for crying out loud! As she surmised the situation, Mae shook her head at the loss. *It's ruined. Second time I've done that! John is going to be furious. Too expensive to replace now, have to wait until I'm home.*

Now she really had to hurry to make that tour!

DR. STAN ANDERS' APARTMENT
ATLANTA
SATURDAY AFTERNOON

Warren stood in his friend's apartment, his face twisted in disgust. The room told the tale of a man on the run. The refrigerator, and closets were empty; items Warren knew were special to Stan were in boxes. There was a distinct food smell, *garlic? Fish?* Someone had been there. He began to prowl.

What, what is this? Warren studied a table with a map of the United States spread across it, with push pins marking different cities. Otherwise, the rooms were empty and revealed no other clues.

The highway miles were tedious back to Lynchburg. Weary, and three days without calling, Warren Peterson pulled into his circle drive, and looked up at his four-bedroom, seven-bathroom villa overlooking the country club. The house had Brazilian cherry floors, and five fireplaces, security system, sound systems, spa, and pool. What was he, a supposed humble minister, doing with all this wealth? His wife and he had grown so far apart. Then it hit him.

The push pins on the U.S. map in Stan's apartment match Stan's travel reports.

A FALSE PROPHET'S ATTEMPT AT REDEMPTION

Stan had two missions. Get to Lynchburg to warn Warren and Connie, then fly to Istanbul to stop the insanity, and decline the money.

What he didn't know was the Turkish terrorist organization was already in Lynchburg.

THE WHISTLEBLOWER
BIRMINGHAM, AL

Danielle Ashton had as many friends keeping close observation on Congressman Shaw as Shaw had watching Danielle.

She and the Congressman were to meet at their secret place in the restaurant at the Airport Top of the Crown Hotel, the following afternoon. The FBI would be listening in.

Terrified at what must be done, Danielle studied her wardrobe evaluating what outfit would best hide the wire. Serendipity would have it, the dress Frank always commented he liked on her, was best for the task at hand. Danielle smiled at the irony, and something as simple as that dress, gave her courage.

When the dreaded luncheon came, it was easy to lead him into the discussion of their illegal acts. He had planned to have the same conversation with her anyway. Words of incrimination flowed freely, and he hung himself with the rope she strategically let out.

When their meal was served, lobster bisque and a Filet mignon, rare, Frank's favorite, Danielle laid down her aces. She explained she had given testimony, and evidence implicating others, in exchange for witness protection. She would go free.

As the two FBI agents approached, she got up from the table, walked away and didn't look back.

****

"I'm ready," Danielle said to the female FBI agent assigned to her. "I've followed your instructions, and only have items that can't be tied to my life here," she added.

Danielle took one last look at her beautiful penthouse with its expensive antiques, and knew her mother would be proud. She felt comfortable in her $20 faded jeans, and her "save the whales" t-shirt. Her clipped and unpolished nails were, for once, not a nuisance. She felt comfortable wearing her mother's one piece of jewelry, a ring with a small ruby. She felt comfortable with her hair pulled back, not recently from the salon. Danielle Ashton prayed, *Lord, that was a close one!*

"By the way, Ms. Ashton, your new name is all we will use from this time forward. I've been meaning to ask you, a wild hunch, you didn't happen to have received *a letter* having to do with doing away with a few politicians, did you?"

"Who, me ???" Danielle answered.

THE GRAND BEACH HOTEL
TEL AVIV
SATURDAY EVENING

Mae stood in the doorway of her hotel room. "Yike. This IS my room," she said. *Am I alone? No one behind the bathroom door. No one under the bed.*

Drawers had been pulled out, and clothes strewn across the room. The side tables were upside down, bathroom countertops swiped clean. Mae backed out of the room. *This is my room number. Those are my clothes.*

"Front Desk—this is Mrs. Lancaster in Room 1108. I need Security to my room immediately. I've been robbed!"

The hotel private security did call in an Israeli official, as no small incident was swept under the rug with the Israeli Police. "Again, please accept our apologies, Mrs. Lancaster. We can't imagine who would do such a thing! You say nothing was taken?"

"No, No. Nothing was taken." Mae stalled, and looked at the floor.

After additional questioning, the hotel management transferred Mae to another room.

✳✳✳✳✳✳✳✳✳✳✳✳

Alone in a new room, Mae took the CD out of her shoulder bag, and sat on the new bed, dumbfounded. *Something IS gone. Someone took my laptop. What shall I do? Who can help me?* Mae considered the last person the hotel manager would want to see, would be her.

The travel agent. Lisa Cohen. Yes, Lisa!

LISA COHEN TRAVEL AGENCY
TEL AVIV
SATURDAY LATE

"Lisa, Lisa!" Mae cried over her shoulder as she paid off her taxi.

Who could this be so late? Lisa rolled her eyes as she locked up the travel agency, and turned to recognize one of her tour guests.

"Yes, Mae, I was just leaving, my children need to be picked up in Haifa," the travel agent said, noticing the woman's taxi speed off. *Uh, oh.*

"I'm in trouble," said Mae. "Some guy was stalking me in the elevator at the hotel. I think he followed me! And, and, my room was RANSACKED!"

Lisa had been brought up expecting danger at any time. "My car is over here, come home with me, we'll decide what to do."

The car following Mae's taxi just missed them.

****

In a coffee shop in Haifa, Mae unburdened her soul to this stranger about the meeting with the publisher, and the woman, Connie Bryan, who was frantic, and looking for something Mae accidentally picked up there.

"I've been called a conspiracy theory fanatic; on the other hand, there have been too many coincidences. I'm frightened, my vacation is ruined, and I want to go home," Mae confessed. "But first I need to borrow your computer, and transfer a file onto a flash drive. Can you help me?

AN ANGEL'S CALL HOME
ETERNAL HOUSE OF PUBLISHING OFFICES
SUNDAY MORNING 9:00AM

Connie wore her jeans to the office. She was finally off the phone. Warren was on his way back to the complex after an unpleasant trip to Atlanta and an equally unpleasant interlude with his wife. The stupid CD had been found, and was making its way back to them, as per Mae. *So there! Boy, I could use a breath of fresh air!*

The vertical blinds to her office balcony, usually kept closed to let in the exact amount of sunlight, hid a beautiful etched sliding glass door. Most of the time, Connie was too busy working to take advantage of the balcony and view of the back of the building. She slid the vertical blinds to the side, opened the glass door, and stepped out.

The smell of the heavily wooded trees below, and sounds of the birds nesting there, were delightful. As she admired what was going to be a beautiful day, and considered what she was going to say to Warren, she did not hear the man come up behind her.

The feeling of falling was short, before the flash of her life before her eyes began. Connie remained calm, and was surprisingly relieved. She would be in more merciful hands soon.

Before Warren's beloved friend and co-worker hit the ground off the seventh story balcony, the terrorist located Connie's note pad on her desk with Mae's tour group scribbled on it.

****

SUNDAY 11:00AM

As Warren Peterson stood alone in the executive offices of his multi-million dollar publishing company, he tried to remain calm. The smell of fish and garlic, again, hung in the air. "Connie! CONNIE!" The balcony glass door was closed but the blinds were open *that's odd.*

Warren sat down at Connie's desk to see if she had left a note. *Nothing.* Not even her note pad. While he waited for Connie to materialize, he was surprised to see Stan Anders break through the door and skid to a stop. Their eyes met.

Warren stood and demanded, "Where—is—Connie?"

Without a word, Dr. Stan Anders hung his head, backed out and disappeared.

BACK IN THE OZARKS
SUNDAY NOON

Dominique didn't have any of her own obligations pressing, so she decided to stay over at Mae's office-cabin. The dog's needed walking and Mae wouldn't be back from her Israel trip for another week. The couch was hard as a rock, but it was the right thing to do, help John out a bit.

John was appreciative; that freed him to do some chores. He wanted to repay the gesture. "Hey, Domi, I'm grilling burgers before I go play cards, you're welcome to come over to the house and eat."

"Sounds great," said Domi.

****

"I'll tidy up the kitchen and you can be on your way," offered Dominique, after both enjoyed a huge cheeseburger and crispy hot and salty fries.

"Great! I'll let ya," laughed John, but before he could push his chair back from the table, the phone startled them both.

"Aren't you going to get it? It might be Mae," said Dominique.

John dived for the phone on its third ring.

"Mr. Lancaster? This is Dr. Warren Peterson in Lynchburg, Virginia. I'm trying to locate my secretary. I need your wife's numbers in Israel."

****

After the unnerving telephone call from Dr. Warren Peterson, John found himself, for the second time, attempting to locate his wife halfway around the world. Steady under pressure, he did not lose his patience until his wife didn't answer her cell phone, nor did her voice mail pick up.

"Yes, Mr. Lancaster that is what I said. Mrs. Lancaster's hotel room was burglarized, and she checked out in a rush, in the night," said the front desk clerk at the Grand Beach Hotel.

The shoe has fallen! Still holding the phone long after being disconnected, John turned to face Dominique and said, "No computer disk, no Ms. Bryan, and now, no Mae."

****

John had Mae's contact numbers for easy access, and was speaking with travel agent Lisa Cohen within minutes.

"No, Mr. Lancaster, not Kansas City, Missouri," said Lisa. "Your wife changed her return flight to go through Lynchburg, Virginia. I put her on the plane myself."

The antique grandfather clock his mother gave him clanged in the background. "*Hummm, I never heard mother's clock before,*" he noted as his stomach soured.

No sooner did John put the phone down than it rang again. "Mr. Lancaster?" It was Warren Peterson again. "May I come to Missouri? I need to be there when your wife's flight arrives."

"No, sir!" said John. "I'm coming to you! She's on her way there! My wife is on her way to Lynchburg."

****

John's gun was not for sport shooting, a Taurus 445 Ultra-Lite .44 Special Revolver, with a grip he could get his whole hand around. This gun's chief purpose was to make large holes, in bodies, at short range.

John's friend picked up on the first ring.

"Bud, I need to get to Virginia today, tonight, or tomorrow. I need to bring my gun. Can you call Phil Hanson and see if he'll fly me? I'll pay him."

"Of course," said Bud, with no questions asked.

LANGLEY

"The missing senator and the governor from Wisconsin have been found, sir," reported Counterintelligence Specialist Lon Munson to CIA Director Carter Elliott. "Not good news. Their bodies were found by hikers up at Timms Hill, Wisconsin; two broken necks. Crime scene photos are identifying tire tracks, could be a limousine."

The CIA Director belted, "Good news? GOOD NEWS? Can we expect ANY GOOD NEWS, Agent Munson?"

"Nothing good from Wisconsin, sir, but something has opened up in Atlanta; a terrorist cell has been activated. I am on my way there now."

ALZHEIMERS UNIT
MADISON, WI

Wisconsin Union Manager, Drayton Morris, returned the borrowed limousine to its fleet, and tossed the gloves into the driver's seat. HIS prints would not be found in there.

A nurse at the Alzheimer's Care Center was waiting for him at the hospital's front entrance. Concerned, the caregiver said, "Mr. Morris, you mustn't leave the building without telling us, sir."

Drayton Morris nodded in agreement, and then proceeded to forget, indeed, about anyone, or anything to do with politics.

MS. CUTESY'S GOOD FORTUNE
AUSTIN, TX

Mrs. David Dunning, otherwise known as Cutesy, cooed and greeted her husband, "Hi, Honey Bunny." Dressed up in everything good taste and high society would find inappropriate, the oil tycoon followed his wife into the living area of their six-bedroom home. Awarded "House of the Year" by the Austin Home Association, the twelve-acre property included an award-winning Japanese garden, and had been featured in *Forbes*.

"You have men waiting for you in our living room, *darlin', THE FBI, darlin','*" she warned in a pronounced southern drawl.

"Mr. Dunning, there have been allegations by the Oil and Gas Historical Society that funds are missing. An IRS Audit has been requested. Normally, the Corpus Christie Police Department would handle this kind of theft; however, how well do you know Judge Isaiah Oakley?" the FBI agent inquired, without emotion.

"I do not know the man," denied Dunning as he meandered over to his built-in bar, and wall of liquor behind it. He poured himself a Scotch, and continued, "I met him once or twice on a few fund-raisers, that is all."

"Gee, Mr. Dunning, your lovely wife, here, Ms. Cutesy, has already told us, Judge Oakley comes to dinner *just all the time,"* the agent said, mimicking her southern accent.

All eyes were on Mrs. David Dunning.

"Sorry, Honey Bunny," said Cutesy, already planning on how to spend all his money.

LYNCHBURG REGIONAL AIRPORT
MONDAY, 6:00AM

The Lynchburg Regional Airport terminals opened at four o'clock in the morning. Warren was there waiting at the west end near the smaller hangers, as the small plane landed.

After brief and polite introductions between John and Warren, John introduced Phil.

Warren said, "Phil, you're welcome to stay. I have standing rooms at the Marriott, and it is no problem. You should rest."

The pilot replied, "Thanks, guys, but all I need is breakfast. It will be a couple of hours until the Cessna is refueled, and that's all I'll need to take back to the air. You two get on with what you need to do. John, call me and I'll pick you up, really, I'll be glad to."

After good lucks and well wishes, Phil gave John the thumb's up, and John thanked Phil, again.

****

"We'll drive straight to the publishing complex. Maybe my secretary will show up with your wife. Or, maybe your wife will show up with my secretary," Warren continued. "If the women do not show by nightfall, we'll go to the police."

John was in no mood to listen to another man bark orders, nevertheless, he agreed. "Okay, we'll go with that." Carrying a duffel bag with underwear and socks, and the Taurus .44, John asked, "Do we know anything new?"

Warren began. "Well, Connie's office feels odd, but I don't know why. I haven't searched the entire complex yet; we can do that together while we wait for Mae's flight this afternoon. A friend is in some kind of trouble. I think he is the cause of something bad, but I don't know what. His name is Stan Anders, and he hit me over the head, and locked me in a storage room a few days ago."

John's eyes narrowed, and fixed on Warren. "Go on."

"I know I should have called the police right away, but this man and I have been friends a long time, and I can't get my head around the strange guy he has become," Warren stopped to take a breath.

"What's on the computer disk?" John asked, man of few words.

"I don't know. Names and addresses. I had it in my possession a few days before Mae picked it up. It's not her fault, John, just bad timing," said Warren, still not believing the recent events.

"Well, I'm going to tell you right now, if anyone has hurt my wife, I'm going to kill him," said John quietly.

LAGUARDIA AIRPORT
NEW YORK, NY
MONDAY 9:00AM

"Glad I didn't have to stick a flash drive up my butt, or wear a microdot under my contact lenses," Mae said, straight-faced to the lady in front of her as they prepared to deplane. The woman vacated her place in line, and scurried up ahead.

Mae laughed at the woman's stunned expression; then felt guilty. *I hope that woman is not on her way to report me,* Mae thought. *Can't take a joke?*

Her connecting flight to Lynchburg was in Terminal D, the same Delta area her night flight arrived in. There would be a two-hour layover, enough time to find the nearest ladies room.

The shoulder bag thrown together while Lisa was checking her out of the hotel was turned upside down on the lavatory. *Let's see, what do I have in here? Money belt, makeup bag, camera, a few souvenirs, travel deodorant and tooth-brush. Is that ALL I have on me?* Mae began to regret her rash departure. She had left all her clothes. The one piece of apparel Mae owned to her name was the beautiful Hijab heads-carf she had crammed down the side pocket of her shoulder bag. Smoothing out the wrinkles of the exquisite sequined and beaded piece of Mediterranean fabric, Mae held it to her face.

"Oh, it's gorgeous." She admired the woman in the mirror. *Should I?*

After a good hour of hiding in the women's lounge, a refreshed Mae exited the ladies room with her head held high, wearing a beautiful turquoise beaded scarf around her head and neck. With the sunglasses she dug from the bottom of her bag, and a quick change to an oversized sweater purchased from the airport boutique, she was unrecognizable.

****

Fifteen minutes before boarding, Mae sat in the waiting area. *Had all this been necessary? Could the break-in have been a coincidence?* As Mae questioned if her husband was right, if her paranoia was truly out of control, she recognized the man across the room. *THE SAME MAN IN THE ELEVATOR AT THE BEACH HOTEL!*

Oh, my God! It IS him. Mae's arms felt like lead pipes and she saw gray, the color that filled her vision when she was about to vomit. Glued to her seat, she watched another man join him. There were TWO of them, searching for someone. HER. They were searching for HER!

****

Without catching any attention, Mae walked out of Delta Terminal D, maneuvered her way to US Airways Terminal C, and changed her boarding pass; to where, she didn't know, and boarded a plane.

The senior flight attendant began his routine:

"Welcome to U.S. Airways Flight 722, we are happy you are flying with us today. Our destination is Greensboro, North Carolina, where the temperature is sixty degrees. If you are not going to Greensboro, you may deplane at this time."

As the plane began its taxi, Mae motioned to the flight attendant, "I'm going to need a drink. Make it two."

"What would you care to drink, Miss?" asked the amused attendant.

"Anything, you pick, I want to relax," said Mae, as she pulled the blanket under her chin, already grabbed from the overhead compartment.

PIEDMONT TRIAD INTERATIONAL
AIRPORT
GREENSBORO, NC
MONDAY, 2:00PM

Mae carefully folded the beautiful heads-
carf. *Sometimes bad men turn out to be good men,
and good men turn out bad men. By their fruits you
will know them, and all that jazz, and I ran for a
reason, didn't I?*

The US Airways flight prepared for landing.
She looked out her window seat as the enor-
mous airport hotels came into view. *John. John.
I'll never leave again.*

Weak with hunger, feeling confident she had
not been followed, Mae's destination became
the vending machines. She pouted as she passed
the baggage claim carousels. *Won't need to stop
there, after all MY clothes are somewhere in a trash
bin in Israel.* Disgusted, Mae continued to brood.
The cell phone toilet episode – no cell phone. "Aren't
there any regular old pay phones anymore?"
Mae complained to an uninterested passer-by.

She looked down at her shoulder bag as if
she hated it. *Is there any money or coins, at the
bottom of this thing?* Once again rummaging,
Mae spotted the flash drive under the fold of the
lining. *Oh, yeah, that's why I'm..., where? North
Carolina.*

A city and state as foreign to Mae Lancaster
as the Via Dolorosa.

****

Packed with a three-day supply of candy bars, and cheese crackers, and two cold Cokes, Mae pulled out her debit card for the umpteenth time at the rental car counter. *Maybe John will know something is wrong when he checks the bank balance.* Mae tried to visualize her husband's face when their bank account reflected about zero by now. She decided against calling her cranky husband until this CD, a flash drive now, was out of her life, and good riddance.

The GPS directed her to Hwy 29, Greensboro into Lynchburg approximately 120 miles and two-and-a-half hours straight north. *I can be there by dark and sleep in my car if I have to, no, too scary. I'll have to find a Motel 6, or 8, or 7, or whatever they are.*

A determined Mae set out to find Connie. The same Connie Bryan whose body lay crumpled, and hidden in the trees, below a seventh story balcony at the publishing house she once hoped would publish her work.

ISTANBUL, TURKEY
END OF THE LINE

"Sit down, Meester Anders," said Sarp Asker, with venom in his voice. The ugliest, meanest, sneakiest Middle Easterner you could imagine, spoke.

Stan looked like prey to the slaughter as he waited in the plush Turkish parlor. They were two religious fanatics from two different religions, each with their own agendas, and each in error. In a rumpled suit and looking ridiculous in this place of opulence, Stan swallowed, and sat down.

"You have done a fine job, Meester Anders," the morally offensive man continued. "I congratulate you for all the reports I have been hearing. There have been many terminations. Still, your government has not been alarmed."

The evil man continued in sarcasm. "Could it be possible to eliminate the entire United States of America Congress and no one notice? Now THAT does give new meaning to the phrase, no one minding the store," he chuckled. The dark man in a black hooded Jubbah became serious.

"Yes, the time has come the United States went away, preferably without a war. Their spirit of greed, control, and covetousness will bring them down. All we need to do is cater to their weaknesses, their arrogance, their unbelievable stupidity, and remove a few key people, of course. Thanks to you, the deed is under way."

The man of great wealth concluded the interview, wearing the mask of a million dollar smile. "Meester Anders, your money is well deserved. There is a suitcase in the hallway on your way out. We will call you."

By the time Stan glanced toward the door and back again, Sarp Asker was gone. He never had a chance to explain why he had come, to stop the insanity, and decline the money.

Dr. Stan Anders also didn't make it to the hallway; there were special back doors for these kinds of deals.

J. EDGAR HOOVER BUILDING
WASHINGTON, DC

"Of the 12,996 murder victims in 2010, of which data was received, 77.4% were male;

"Concerning murder victims whose race is known, it is about 50.4% Black and 47.0% White with 2.6% other races;

"Single victim/single offender situations account for about 48.4% of all murders;

"67.5% involve firearms;

"53.0% are killed by someone they know;

"37.5% female victims are murdered by their husbands or boyfriends;

"41.8% of victims were murdered during arguments;

"Murder by race, sex, age, weapons — we have every statistic imaginable.

But what I want to know is, if it will not be too much trouble, HOW MANY CONGRESSMEN AND JUDGES HAVE DIED IN THE LAST THIRTY, SIXTY, AND NINETY DAYS? AND, I WANT TO KNOW WHY, AND HOW," howled FBI Director Matthew Conway. "And, I want to know NOW!"

LANGLEY

The CIA in Atlanta knew about, and had been watching the sleeper cell for years, doing nothing until there was evidence it had been activated. Information had been uncovered, an execution cell had been brought in, and a portable field office had been set up.

Germany's Interior Minister had been working closely with American CIA to gather information about possible right-wing extremists in both their countries. Counterterrorist Specialist Lon Munson had been assigned to monitor neo-Nazi groups in Germany with ties back to the United States; however, the Director of the CIA pulled Agent Munson off Germany, to address the Atlanta activity.

THE WHITE HOUSE

"Mr. Prime Minister, Khaleel" President Saundra Adams addressed the Prime Minister of Turkey after the customary protocol. "What do you have for me?"

"Someone dangerous causing a great deal of trouble to Turkey is coming your way," replied Prime Minister Khuzaymah.

"Atlanta?"

"No, Lynchburg, Virginia. What goes on in Lynchburg, Virginia, Madam President?" the Prime Minister asked, perplexed.

"Nothing we are aware of, big religious goings on there, I think. Thank you, sir, you have been helpful to the United States." President Adams disconnected her direct line.

Religion. The realization came to President Saundra Adams slowly. *The assassinations are connected by two major religions.*

****

Secret Service Agent Glenda Wiley had been standing at her post outside the Oval Office several hours when the door opened a bit.

"Agent Wiley, prepare for an unannounced visit over to the CIA."

"Madam President, you know how I hate it when you do that to me," the exasperated FBI agent complained.

"I find out more when it's a surprise. I don't know if I am in or out of their loop." The President rarely had to explain herself, but this was different. She trusted Glenda Wiley to transport her there and back, safe and unnoticed.

"Well, okay, even my ten-year-old daughter has been printing obituaries off the Internet of an alarming number of dead U.S. politicians."

ETERNAL HOUSE OF PUBLISHING
MONDAY NOON

Although publishing and printing had changed to the desktop, deadlines and production schedules had not changed. The place just could not be shut down without notice. Because Warren was well-respected, there were no concerns when he announced the complex would be closed. All offices were dark as the two men checked corridors and empty rooms. They found nothing.

"Let's wait in the cafeteria until it is time to go back to the airport, where we can get something to eat," said Warren.

Food was the furthest thing from Warren's mind, but his belt closed two notches smaller, and he felt weak.

The vending machine tuna on rye tasted better than he thought. He washed the sandwich down with an orange soda, and walked around with his mind on the fact Connie's Trailblazer was in her parking spot. *Who could she be with?*

John wasn't eating, but handling a gun at a nearby lunch table.

Alarmed, Warren asked, "What are you going to do with that?"

The quiet guy across the room was loading bullets. "I hope nothing," said John.

"My wife's flight lands in one hour."

With his gun ready in the pocket of his jacket, John opened his sandwich, ham and Swiss, glanced at it, and tossed it into the trash bin.

****

"Well, it's time to go back to the airport," Warren alerted John. "The connecting Delta flight out of LaGuardia will be here soon. Mae will deplane, and Connie will be there waiting for her, too. This nightmare will be over," Warren stated, as convincingly as he could.

For the second time that day, Warren Peterson's Lincoln Town Car sped off to the Lynchburg Regional Airport where Mae Lancaster proceeded to NOT get off the plane.

****

Every closet and stairwell had been searched. Connie's car was still in the lot; Mae's cell phone still not picking up.

John was antsy as he spotted the guest phone on a nearby conference table. "Do I need to dial nine?" he asked, and pulled a wallet-sized address book from his shirt pocket.

"No, that's an outside line," said Warren. "Have an idea?"

"I'm going to call Lisa Cohen again," said John. "She's the quickest way to find out how to trace someone."

****

Warren returned from his private men's room with his hair combed and shirt changed. "What in the world??" With his jaw hanging open, he gaped at John.

"She didn't make her connection in New York." John said, holding his hand, his knuckles bloodied.

"Well, we knew THAT," said Warren, staring at the hole in his conference room wall.

****

"Come with me!" Warren shouted. "There's another place to search. I didn't think of going back to the grounds maintenance area. I should have," he said, browbeating himself.

THE COMPLEX GROUNDS
MONDAY, 6:00PM

Mae pulled her white Ford Focus rental into the empty parking lot of the publishing complex at a crawl. The last time she had been here, the lot was full of cars. Connie's Trailblazer was easy to find, up front in the "reserved for Connie Bryan" space. She pulled in next to it; the only other car the big Lincoln several spaces down from Connie's.

I think I'll leave my bag in the car, thought Mae, as she slipped the flash drive into her pocket. She locked the car and snapped her car keys onto her belt loop, and headed toward the main building.

****

Dang, its dark out here. Doesn't anybody believe in street lights around here? Mae could hear her heart in her temples. *Should have wore my glasses, can't make out the steps.*

The front door of the main office was locked. *Stupid! Stupid! Stupid! Why didn't I call ahead? Why did I assume someone would be here? Wasn't this a work day? Where is the second shift?*

The publishing company spent a fortune on landscaping. Mae walked through painstakingly cared-for fountains, and outdoor sculptures. She strolled through tiled patios with

157

picnic tables, and admired beautiful ironwork until she came to the heavily wooded back of the building; the very dark back of the building.

I think I better go back to the rose garden. Mae started to backtrack. *At least you can see the lights from the parking lot there.* Just when her confidence began to return, she stopped dead in her tracks. *What was that noise? Someone down there by that statue! Should I call out? No, go back to the rear of the building into the trees, and get a better look.*

Two men, three men, FOUR MEN! Mae didn't need her glasses to recognize the men stalking her, hunting her all the way across the Atlantic for what she had in her pocket. With the resolve of a veteran spy, church secretary Mae Lancaster, quiet as a church mouse, backed up, backed up, and crouched down, lower, lower alongside the building where she would be hidden. *Whoa, what is that smell? Kind of foul. What is that over there? A log? A rock? No, not a log, not a rock, no, no, it's, it's Connie!*

GROUNDSKEEPER'S GARAGE

The groundskeeper's office side door opened onto an outdoor sidewalk that led to a large metal building with giant overhead doors. Dusk was upon them.

"This sidewalk leads to a separate building for mowers and tractors," said Warren, as the two men stepped into the evening air. As they approached the garage entrance, Warren jerked his head around and whispered, "Hide!"

Each man dove to separate sides of the walkway, John behind a trash barrel, and Warren behind park bench. John drew his weapon.

"I saw a flashlight bouncing around in there," said Warren between his teeth. "Don't let that thing go off," he added, pointing to John's gun.

"Worry about you," John warned, in control of his weapon and his emotions.

As the two men prepared themselves to enter the garage, a Special FBI Tactics Team materialized. Dr. Warren Peterson and John Lancaster from the Missouri Ozarks were on the ground, silenced, de-armed, and whisked away within fifteen seconds.

FBI MOBILE TASK UNIT

Held in the nearby FBI mobile unit, the shocked men were de-briefed. FBI moved in the shadows all around the complex. Warren was telling all he knew, and John, as usual, remained quiet.

"You say this man's wife has a computer disk with information on it that might be at the heart of this matter?" an FBI interrogator demanded of Warren.

"Well, yes." Warren stole a look over at John, and received a go-ahead nod to continue. "I copied the disk off of my co-worker's computer, my friend Stan Anders, Dr. Stan Anders. It was a list of names, cities and states, that's all I know."

"Then my wife, Mae, picked up the disk, and took it with her on vacation," added John.

THE PURSUIT
THE COMPLEX GROUNDS

Mae's eyes stung; her energy gave out, and she remained on her knees. *Oh, Connie. Oh, Connie.* Connie Bryan's eyes were closed, and her body badly broken. The weather had been cool; the scene undisturbed; the sight could have been a lot worse.

Oh, Connie, what has been done here? Mae's eyes moved upward to where Connie's spirit would be, if it had been lingering there, in the air. Could it be possible her spirit was still near? *We even talked about the supernatural and such things,* Mae remembered. "We're not defeated yet, dear lady," Mae whispered.

She reached down into her pocket to touch the flash drive. Mae made a promise to Connie, God, and everyone; she would deliver what was on this flash drive to the authorities, or die trying. *Why do you love us, Lord? We are so wicked.*

No longer afraid of the men in black, Mae began to stir. She needed a plan, and quick. *Well, I can't stay here or they will find me.* She looked around. *No noise. I have to get back to my car! Yes, I'm getting the hell out of this blankety blank place!*

BACK AT THE MOBILE FBI UNIT

The two men had been sitting alone without speaking when an FBI Agent climbed into the task force vehicle, and in a matter-of-fact tone announced, "a woman has been found dead on the grounds."

Warren swayed, falling out of his chair onto the floor.

John charged the unprepared FBI Agent, and landed a swift blow to the head; grabbed both the agent's gun, and his own gun that had been left out in full view. Over his shoulder, he determined Warren would be of no use to him.

After a short struggle with the heavy metal vehicle door, John dropped to the ground, and disappeared into night.

****

Operations Agent Kamber Jeanes was furious at her subordinate. "What am I working here with, a bunch of idiots? Okay, what do we have?" the seasoned agent harshly addressed the whole team.

"Another car arrived in the executive parking area. A Ford Focus rented by Mae Lancaster. She is on the grounds."

Warren scooted his chair back into a corner, and covered his head with his hands. He didn't need to be informed the dead woman found on the grounds was the love of his life, Connie Bryan.

****

"This is what we're going to do," directed Agent Jeanes. "We're going to lure whoever is in this complex to a single point. Team One will locate and secure Mr. Lancaster, AGAIN. Team Two's mission is to apprehend Mrs. Lancaster, and obtain the CD. The Strike Team will take the Executive Offices where Team One and Team Two will serve as bait. Let me be clear, do NOT engage our terrorists. I want living, breathing assailants, if possible.

"I thought you said every good terrorist is a dead terrorist," commented a strike team agent, thinking he was making a joke.

"Well, at least ONE alive, anyway," the head FBI Agent concluded, with a wry smile.

A HUSBAND'S SEARCH

John surveyed his surroundings. *What harm would it have done to be a little nicer? I have never been happier in my life as when I am with her.* He was surprised at his own revelation. *I shouldn't have complained about all the animals, it isn't that big of a deal. She is my everything....*

He circled the complex twice, and counted six dangerous men, Middle Eastern in descent, wearing black and carrying automatic weapons. *Where is the FBI? What are they up to? They are good at staying out of sight, or, are nowhere to be found. It figures!*

In the rose garden, behind a stone arbor, John paused to catch his breath, and shake out his aching, gun-gripping hand. On the other side of the garden stood the black iron gate that led down into the parking lot. He straightened his spine to peer over the gate, and saw three lone cars down there. *Hadn't there only been two?*

THE FAITH OF MAE

Mae watched three of her pursuers leave the rose garden, and walk off toward the executive office building. *Could I be so lucky? There's still another man out there somewhere,* she calculated.

There was no way through to the parking lot without crossing the rose garden, and down through the iron gate, or, she could climb over the fence. With her eyes drifting up to the tall fence with sharp points on top of it, she decided against it. *Impossible!* She shuddered, and made her decision. *I'll walk right through that gate as walking into a lion's den. The lions are either going to eat me, or God will have closed their mouths.*

Through the gate and down the steps, she could see her car. Down, down; a few more steps. Ankle turned; she stumbled. A yelp escaped her. *That hurt! Almost there. Closer! Closer!*

Her keys were in the lock.

I WAS LOST, AND THEN I WAS FOUND

John retreated into the shelter of the trees. *Was it those men, or FBI?* He fastened his eyes on the spot from where the sound had come. He dropped his gun to his side, and felt his chest and shoulders relax. Mae approached the black wrought iron gate as though she didn't have a care in the world.

It took all of John's will to hold back, and not run to her. If his wife saw him, she would call out, maybe make a scene.

Shaken back to the awareness of danger, he lifted his gun back up to position. *Doesn't she know the whole world has been looking for her? Where has she been? What does she know?* He was wild-eyed by now.

I've got to follow her, get her out of the way, and keep her quiet. He was well aware keeping his wife quiet was going to be the bigger of the feats.

The fence was tall, even dangerous, but doable.

THE OFFICE PARKING LOT

Slouched down, with the car doors locked, Mae popped up to check the back seat. She took a breath. *No one.* A quick scan told her the car was as she had left it. Candy wrappers were as they had fallen.

Without a minute to lose, and clueless on finding the nearest police station, no phone, and no one to trust, Mae's hand felt for the key in the ignition. With her eyes in the rear view mirror she prepared to turn the key.

Tap, tap, tap.

Mae's stomach sunk to her feet. Someone was at her side window. A big shadow at her window! She was dead. She was going to die. *I love you, John, I'm sorry. Don't look over, don't look over.*

Tap, tap, tap.

Mae turned to face her fate.

✱✱✱✱✱✱✱✱✱✱✱✱

"Let me in," John said, motioning urgently for her to comply. "Hurry Mae, hurry!"

As she bit back the tears and gasped for air, Mae hit the unlock button, then hit the lock button. After two or three times of the locks going up and down, up and down, John's eyes, as big as saucers, glared through the glass. When he was able to pull the door open, he scrambled into the car, and placed his lips over hers.

"Holy Moly! "Mae said in amazement.

"Don't say a word. We'll talk later. Right now we have to find the FBI."

"Noooo, we need the police. My friend is dead, she's been murdered! It's been HOR-RI-BLE! Dreadful, simply dreadful!"

"Noooo, for once listen to me, Mae. The FBI are here. HERE ON THE GROUNDS, looking for us. Our safest bet is the FBI command post. I know where it is, but we have to go now, and we have to be quiet. Can you, Mae? Can you follow me, sweetheart?"

"No," Mae whispered. "Honey, I've hurt my ankle. I can't put my foot down."

****

"Okay, Mae, I'm going to carry you, you can help with your other leg. Do you have the disk?"

"No," said Mae.

"What do you mean, no?" John scanned his wife.

"It's a flash drive now," corrected Mae.

John Lancaster gritted his teeth. "I'm going to get out on my side, and you get out on your side at the same time, low, don't let the door swing open, or close loud. I'll come around, crawl to you. The two of us are going to half-walk, half-run, whatever we have to do to climb that hill over there. We can see the FBI mobile unit from there. Are you ready, honey?"

"Yes, okay," said Mae.

Both doors opened. Mr. and Mrs. John Lancaster rolled out of the car, and lowered their bodies to the ground. For the second time, John was on the ground, silenced, de-armed, and whisked away by the FBI within fifteen seconds.

He didn't mind so much this time, however, because the look on his wife's face, as she too was apprehended, was priceless.

THE WRAP-UP

It didn't take long for the FBI to seize, detain, and remove six Turkish terrorists from the scene, four dead, two alive.

By the time the sun came up, it was if the events hadn't happened, except the sun didn't come up for Connie Bryan.

Warren Peterson was driven away in an ambulance; the FBI would meet with Peterson again, after a medical exam.

FBI Agent Jeanes was to report the information found on the elusive CD tied to an international terrorist cell. The church secretary from the Missouri Ozarks kept her promise to her friend, Connie Bryan, by delivering the flash drive into the agent's hands.

"Mrs. Lancaster, have you viewed what's on the flash drive?" The agent directed the question to Mae, as the flash drive was inserted into the mobile command unit's computer. The strike team and John looked on.

"Yes, Ma'am," said Mae. "It is a mail merge document. Mail merge documents are used to send letters out. Every secretary can identify one. The names and addresses on the flash drive belong with *a letter* of some kind."

You could hear a pin drop, then CHAOS!

KAUAI, HI

When retired U.S. Army Special Forces Glenn E. Colton selected his first boat for off-shore cruising in 1976, he had no idea what part his sailing ability would play in an unexpected early retirement.

The Madam DuBarry was anchored off the shore of the Dry and Wet Caves of Kauai, Hawaiian Islands, where the largest lighthouse of its kind resided. By transferring all their assets to cash, and building false identities, two life-long friends had all they needed for the years they had left.

Colton's routine included the sports and business sections in the *Honolulu Star-Advertiser*, and especially the obituaries. Bodies, both dead and alive, were surfacing. Investigations into political corruption in bribery, extortion, embez-zlement, arms trafficking, money laundering and bank fraud were all in the news. Of special interest to him was the news of the California Senator who masterminded an arms trafficking ring, and had been *"presumably killed by his part-ners south of the border,"* the article reported.

"Let's see, what fruit shall I have for break-fast today?" Colton closed his laptop, and began another day in Paradise for an elderly guy with leg braces, learning how to hula.

FEDERAL CORRECTIONAL INSTITUTION
ASHLAND, KY

Ray Bucks Derrick held all the markers Supreme Court Chief Justice Thom Hopkins owed the Mob, and this would be his ticket to beat the rap of hiring an arsonist to get rid of the double-crossing judge.

Question: What do lawyers and judges do all day?

Answer: Make deals, of course.

That was exactly what Derrick did. Both the state and federal Attorney Generals did not want the entire business to come out about the gambling Chief Justice. Who knew how many cases would be affected? It was decided to obtain the information from the ponies man for a reduced sentence, then, go after the judge's accomplices.

In one of the lowest security prisons, well known for their wellness programs, including aerobic exercise and stress reduction, Derrick did quite well for himself. He was getting away from the Kentucky Horse Racing Commission breathing down his neck, and there could even be a book deal.

Oh, the irony of justice.

FEDERAL MEDICAL CENTER
LEXINGTON, KY

The Federal Medical Center in Lexington houses 1,464 male inmates at high security. The building built in 1935 on 1,000 acres under the name *United States Narcotic Farm* was originally opened to be both prison and hospital with its agenda to study drug addicts. In 1974, the institution became a federal prison, yet maintained its psychiatric hospital. That was where the arsonist Joel L. Moore belonged; creepy place, creepy person.

"Whatever you do," said the prison physician. "Don't give him any matches!"

THE WALL STREET BROTHER
BOCA RATON, FL

When Harry Walden received the coded message from his panic-stricken sister, he knew he slipped up somewhere. He either left a fingerprint, or a clue. *I shouldn't have left the picture of the girl,* he admonished himself. *Couldn't resist rubbing it in. Well, I can't show up at the hardware store. The FBI will be waiting. Let's see, Plan B, Plan B.*

On a safe phone line, Harry Walden called in a favor from a banker in Boca. After all, Harry Walden maneuvered money, people, and circumstances as easily as others counted to ten.

****

Harry Walden shadowed the banker to his car.

"Harry, we heard you were out," said the money man. "I want to thank you for covering for us. What's up? Is something wrong?"

"My sister is in trouble. It will go better for her if I am not available," explained Walden. "Don't worry, nothing to do with banking, but I need to leave the country, what do you say?"

"What about Fort Frances, Ontario? I own property there," replied the banker.

"Perfect. You can consider us even." Harry Walden obviously wasn't going to say anything about the missing governor.

BOCA RATON, FL

"Excuse me." The teenager bumped into Barbara Jones in the grocery checkout, and slipped her the note.

"The Hardware Store is being watched, Brother Harry went off shore, Brother sorry. Will be in touch, keep to story you know nothing. You'll be OK, keep to story you know nothing. Love, H."

"I'm going to kill him," said Barbara. "He's dragged me into something, and left again."

As it turned out, it was the best thing her brother Harry could have done.

****

"Mom, there is a man at the front door." Out of breath, Randie Jones ran through the house.

Barbara had been waiting for her brother's shenanigans to come knocking. With one last look in the mirror, to put on her steel and determined face, she said, "Okay, honey, I'm coming, wait in your room."

A tailored, silver-haired gentleman stood on her front stoop with a chauffeur, and a dark green Jaguar in the drive. "I have come to meet my granddaughter, Ms. Jones. I have come to say how sorry I am the two of you have lived alone these years. My son is dead.

There have been grave mistakes made. I have come to tell you, you and the child have a family. We want you to be a part of our family, *your family."*

NEW BEGINNINGS

It was possible to leave your mistakes behind, and start over with a clean sheet, even if you weren't in the Witness Protection Program.

"The dinosaur fossil beds from the Jurassic Period were discovered in 1909," recited Louise Logan as she began her tour group. "Thousands of fossils have been shipped to museums," she continued.

Her new job at the Dinosaur National Monument, located on the border of Colorado and Utah where the Green and Yampa Rivers met, was a dream come true for Danielle Ashton, alias Louise Logan. Her ability to close a deal came in handy working for conservation politics, organizations put in place to protect the environment against powerful members of Congress who would compromise free-flowing rivers and scenic canyons.

The gorgeous head-turning Danielle Ashton, now plain Louise Logan, headed home after work to beautiful, and tiny, Elk Springs, the unincorporated town in Moffat County, Colorado, in the middle of nowhere, and she couldn't be happier.

THE LAST FUNERAL
TEXAS STATE CEMETERY
AUSTIN, TX

The *Cleaning of the House* that turned out to be plain old vigilante justice and old-fashioned greed was coming to a close.

Surrounded by Secret Service agents, the President of the United States expressed her personal condolences to the family of the Governor of Texas for his untimely heart attack. *Guilt, fear and stress can really kill a guy,* the President pondered. *Better reinstate my morning prayer time.*

As they returned to their vehicles, Secret Service Agent Glenda Wiley addressed the President. "Did we find out who this minister was, Ma'am?"

The President sighed. "They are still filling in the blanks. What we do know is a disturbed Protestant minister decided the best way to create a holier America was to eliminate its leaders. This deeply religious man then teamed up with our international enemies, who had an agenda of their own for THEIR god and country," President Adams added. "It appears the minister had been recruited."

"What about the woman in Missouri, she going to keep quiet?" Agent Wiley knew it was not her business, but valued her private conversations with the President.

179

"I have asked for the woman's file, I want to know what she reads, what she does for income, what she will do next after what most would consider a life-changing experience."

LANGLEY

The Case of the Murdered Church Secretary, as the operation became code-named, was solved before the United States had no one left to fill the United States capitol.

"How many of the fifteen thousand names and addresses found on the list have been neutralized?" the CIA Director challenged his right-hand man.

CIA Special Agent Lon Munson had been gathering information and statistics without rest. "Fourteen thousand of *the letters* were thrown in the trash as a hoax, sir. The people asked us some questions, and we received a few lectures, but nothing needing to be watched. Two hundred twelve letters went to addresses unknown, undeliverable; six hundred and forty residences still had the letter. After a visit from the FBI, those threats have also been eliminated. There are one hundred eleven viable threats remaining, now in play, or may go into play. We lost twelve Senators, twenty House Representatives, and five judges. Of the thirty-seven deaths, fourteen are homicides, and twenty-three are suspicious deaths. It has been quite a plot to unravel, sir."

"Good work, Agent Munson."

Agent Munson turned and rested his hand on the doorknob. "Sir? You don't suppose any of the letter recipients distributed copies, and who knows how many letters are REALLY out there..."

ALEXANDRIA NATIONAL CEMETERY
ALEXANDRIA CITY, VA

The funeral procession for Ms. Connie Bryan was bumper to bumper. Connie Bryan's love for others and her wonderful reputation reached back two decades. Her daughter from California had come and gone, as had most of her publishing friends. Four persons remained: Dr. Warren Peterson and his wife, Julie, and Mae and John Lancaster. The two couples, drawn together by a devastating course of events, each stood with their own thoughts:

I'm glad to have my husband back, but the cost was too great. Mrs. Julie Peterson's lips quivered as she regretted every unkind word she ever said.

I'm glad to have my wife back, it could have been Mae in that box. John Lancaster renewed his vows.

Dr. Warren Peterson had become a different man. *This is not my game anymore. I wonder if the small church in Asheville is still looking for a pastor. And Connie, Connie, will you ever forgive me? Yes, you would say. "Of course, Warren, I forgive you."*

Mae held her husband's hand and let him steady her. *Oh, how lucky I am. How blessed I am. And Connie, I'm sorry we didn't have a chance to finish our conversation on everything from UFOs, to melting ice caps, to just what IS the Kingdom of Heaven. I'll see you on the other side, my friend.*

As the two couples went their separate ways, John caught a movement out of the corner of his eye. CIA Agent Munson appeared, and fell into step beside them.

"The President wants to thank you for your part in helping serve our country, Mrs. Lancaster. She believes there is a company who can help you with one of your product ideas." Agent Munson received two blank faces staring back at him.

"Come again?" John's face grimaced in disbelief. "What do Mae's products have to do with the President?" He got right to the point.

"The President agrees your disposable dish cuffs to keep your sleeves dry while doing dishes may be of interest to DuPont. They will be calling you." And with that, the CIA Agent was gone, and John and Mae Lancaster stood alone in a strange cemetery, quite homesick.

THE WHITE HOUSE

When no one was looking, except the CIA of course, President Saundra Adams loved to put her feet up on the couch in the Oval Office. She closed her eyes, and nightmares of a Sharia kind of government in the United States, where religious men of ANY religion made up their own laws, haunted her thoughts.

Instead of counting sheep, the President drifted down, and counted the good that happened in spite of all the tragedy. *An arms smuggling gang was shut down in Arizona, Alabama's corruptive deal-makings have been held at bay, for now anyway, workers' voices were being heard, and I'll be able to appoint another judge, someone honorable, preferably by the name of 'Deborah.'*

Yet sleep wasn't to come. The President rolled off the couch and strode over to the door where Agent Wiley would be faithfully standing. Through the door she whispered, "Glenda, don't forget to ask me for a package I have for your daughter, Kassi. She was first to realize we were attending too many funerals, leave it to the children to keep us straight. I have a small thank you for her, something from the President."

MISSOURI HILLS

"Dominique, we're RICH, DuPont bought my idea about the wrists cuffs!" Mae knew how outrageous the announcement sounded.

"Yeah, sure, Mae, whatever you say," said Dominique, as she saddled their horses.

Mae didn't try to convince her friend the President of the United States interceded for her in a business deal. Who would believe her, anyway? No one! "Well, I'll just tell you this, Domi, God keeps His promises...He certainly does. By the way, there aren't any storms in the forecast, are there?"

LANCASTER HOME
SUNDAY MORNING

John found himself taking Sunday trips into town for the newspaper. Politicians were coming out of the woodwork to appear on radio talk shows and on evening news broadcasts, making new pledges to the American people. *"Humph!"* He couldn't help be cynical, and wonder how long the new promises would last.

"Mae, how about dinner and a movie, when you get back from church?"

EPILOGUE

CROSS TIMBERS CHURCH
LAKE OZARK, MO
SUNDAY

*A*t three o'clock in the afternoon, Mae went on her rounds. Bibles and hymnals back to the pews, check Fellowship Hall, empty trash, lock pastor's study, leaving all messages taped to his chair. Stopped on her way through the sanctuary to gaze upon her favorite mural, she hummed, *"He Ain't Heavy, He's My Brother."*

She closed up the church, and turned the key in the lock.

THE END

Dearest Reader,

*M*ost of us believe God is in His Heaven and He is working His plan, a plan only He understands... *his ways are not our ways.*

- Noah was saved from destruction because he was a *righteous man* but his subsequent drunkenness led to a curse upon his grandson;
- Abraham spoke with God in intimate fellowship; however his flaws led to doubt and sleeping with his wife's handmaiden;
- God saved Lot from the destruction of Sodom, however he had a friendship with the world that led to incest;
- Moses was not allowed to cross the finish line; even Yahweh's mediator had to stay within certain bounds;
- King David responded with exemplary repentance after Bathsheba, but was denied his dream of building the temple;
- Nebuchadnezzar was seen as the instrument of God, and was called *my servant*, but later he and his descendants were to be punished.

And we could go on. The Apostle Paul knew his righteousness *was but rags,* but it appears our current leaders in politics and religion cannot grasp this precept. The Pharisees were criticized by Jesus for their lack of compassion for the poor, and for their failure to practice what they preached. And our worse downfall was when the people at Jesus trial chose Barabbas, the WRONG ONE! In our day and age God will judge us for what we do for the poor and needy. Not our assemblies and offerings.

I refresh our memory of our shortcomings to remind us God loves us anyway. The reason why our belief system is superior is because we believe a debt has been paid in our behalf.

Our fictional story ends with God keeping His promise, but in truth He always does keep His promises, and that part is Non-fiction.

www.djparsons.com

CPSIA information can be obtained at www.ICGtesting.com
Printed in the USA
LVOW060326210712

290796LV00001B/2/P